FATIMA

Fatima

The Story Behind the Miracles

RENZO AND ROBERTO ALLEGRI

Translated by Gary Seromik

CHARIS

SERVANT PUBLICATIONS
ANN ARBOR, MICHIGAN

Title of the Italian original:
Reportage da Fatima: La storia e i prodigi nel racconto del nipote di suor Lucia
Copyright 2000 by Ancora Editrice, Milan

Charis Books is an imprint of Servant Publications especially designed to serve Roman
Catholics.

Published by Servant Publications
P.O. Box 8617
Ann Arbor, Michigan 48107

Cover design by Eric Walljasper, Minneapolis, MN

02 03 10 9 8 7 6 5 4 3 2 1

Printed in the United States of America
ISBN 1-56955-316-5

To Sr. Lucia of Jesus,
the loving and enthusiastic witness
to a sublime story,
the most fantastic story
that one can imagine,
a story that is full of hope;
and to Fr. José dos Santos Valinho,
who, with loving generosity,
tried to introduce us
to its most true and concrete aspects.
With gratitude and affection.

Contents

A Note on the Third Secret of Fatima

In the brief interval between the original appearance of this book in Italian and its publication now in an English translation, a startling new development took place in the continuing story of Fatima: On May 13, 2000, the Vatican revealed the celebrated "third secret" given by the Blessed Virgin to the young visionaries and recorded later by Sr. Lucia for the pope. The words had been carefully guarded since the time of the apparitions in 1917, but at long last, Pope John Paul II decided to release the text to a public eager to know its meaning.

This "secret" inescapably plays a part in the story presented in this little volume, and the story unfolds on the assumption that the message remains hidden. To complete the picture, then, it seems fitting to offer here the unedited text of the secret's official English translation as issued by Rome.

Sr. Lucia provided an introductory statement about why she recorded the vision, then reported:

After the two parts which I have already explained, at the left of Our Lady and a little above, we saw an Angel with a flaming sword in his left hand; flashing, it gave out flames that looked as though they would set the world on fire; but they died out in contact with the splendour that Our Lady radiated towards him from her right hand: pointing to the earth with his right hand, the Angel cried out in a loud voice: *"Penance, Penance, Penance!"* And we saw in an immense light that is God: "something similar to how people appear in a mirror when they pass in front of it" a Bishop dressed in White "we had the impression that it was the Holy Father." Other Bishops, Priests, men and women Religious going up a steep mountain, at the top of which there was a big Cross of rough-hewn trunks as of a cork-tree with the bark; before reaching there the Holy Father passed through a big city half in ruins and half trembling with halting step, afflicted with pain and sorrow, he prayed for the souls of the corpses he met on his way; having reached the top of the mountain, on his knees at the foot of the big Cross he was killed by a group of soldiers who fired bullets and arrows at him, and in the same way there died one after another the other Bishops, Priests, men and women Religious, and various lay people of different ranks and positions. Beneath the two arms of the Cross there were two Angels each with a crystal aspersorium in his hand, in which they gathered up the blood of the Martyrs and with it sprinkled the souls that were making their way to God.

The full meaning of the message is still debated, but one thing is certain: The Vatican insists that John Paul II is the "bishop dressed in white" who was struck down. The attempt on the Holy Father's life that took place on May 13, 1981, occurred on the anniversary of the first apparition at Fatima. Ever since that day, the Holy Father has remained grateful to the Virgin, firmly convinced that she who prophesied the event also intervened to spare his life.

The revelation of the secret has by no means brought the speculation and debate about its contents to an end. Its terrifying images continue to trouble the imagination of many believers who contemplate the future, even as they jar the memory of countless more who recognize in the vision the horrors of the last century.

Yet the reader who finds this complex picture of blood and fire disturbing has all the more reason to set it in the context of the simple pastoral story told in the following pages. Like stars in the night, the pure, humble spirits of the three shepherd children shine clearly and steadily in the darkness of an unbelieving world. God grant that their example of sacrificial courage will inspire us all to imitation.

The Editor

Preface

This book is the account of an amazing adventure that deeply touched its authors.

When they received word that the two Portuguese shepherd children had been beatified, Renzo Allegri, a prestigious journalist, and his son, Roberto, who is also a journalist, perceived the importance of this event and set off on a journey to Fatima. This town with an Arab (and Muslim) name has been a magnet for Christians ever since the Virgin Mary, who is highly venerated in the Koran, honored it with her presence. There the Blessed Virgin created a prophetic event of enormous importance, which surprised and caught everybody off guard, including many eminent churchmen and theologians.

Spiritual consolation has always characterized apparitions in the past. The great apparitions of modern times stand out vividly in world history.

In 1531, the apparition of Our Lady of Guadalupe in Mexico helped to establish firmly not only the Church in the New World, but also the physical, cultural, and spiritual mixture that is characteristic of Latin America. The Virgin Mary revealed her wishes to the Spanish bishop of the city of the *conquistadores* through a humble Indian.

In 1830, the apparition of Our Lady of the Miraculous Medal in Paris renewed a Church that had been decimated and destroyed by the French Revolution, giving it a new missionary and charismatic impetus.

In 1858, the Blessed Mother sought out Bernadette at Lourdes. There the young girl lived with her family, the poorest family in the village, in an old jail that had been abandoned because it was unfit for human habitation. Her father had even been arrested in 1856, accused of stealing some flour out of hunger.

"People thought he was guilty for stealing the flour," the baker said, "because his life was so miserable," without any other motive or basis.

For this very same reason the Virgin Mary sought out those whom the public authorities attacked because of their poverty. She who is known as the "humble servant" (see Lk 1:38, 48) came to remind the world of the primary *kerygma* of the gospel, "Blessed are the poor" (see Lk 6:20), precisely at the moment when the cry of the bourgeois republic was "Get rich!"

Fatima is without doubt the most prophetic modern apparition. In the very year (1917) when atheistic communism was coming to power in Russia (it eventually extended its dominion over one third of humanity), the Virgin Mary issued a call to prayer for an "end to persecution" and for the "conversion of Russia." Her promise seemed very unlikely, given the dictatorial, military, and police power of such a strong, central regime. I am the first to admit that I was surprised to see this regime collapse internally, contrary to all evidence.

Another surprise also occurred. In spite of Pope Pius XI's traditional reserve, which maintained that a pope should not involve himself in private revelations, Pius XII renewed on four different occasions the consecration of Russia that the Virgin Mary had requested through Lucia. Pope Paul VI commemorated it in a solemn way during the Second Vatican Council on November 21, 1964. John Paul II repeated it another four times up to 1984, involving all the bishops. Then came *perestroika* and the end of the persecutions ...

I could mention several other surprises, which have never ceased to astonish me in my studies of this unusual event. Pius XII was ordained a bishop on May 13, 1917, the day of the first apparition at Fatima. He privately experienced the miracle of the sun in the Vatican Gardens, which accompanied the last apparition on October 13, 1917. The cardinal whom he had appointed as his delegate to the fortieth anniversary celebration of the apparitions revealed this fact to the pilgrims. (The Holy Office immediately published a retraction since this Sacred Congregation at the Vatican did not forget the traditional duty of papal reserve regarding such apparitions.)

Fatima was an adventure for me, too, from the moment when I had to deal with the doubts that an eminent theologian such as Fr. Dhanis methodically raised. It left a deep impression on me for a long time.

When I ventured to respond to an invitation from the Italian radio station RAI 1 on the occasion of the eightieth anniversary of the miracle of the sun (October 13, 1997), I failed to foresee that my few, prudent words would provoke a journalistic scoop: Laurentin reveals the "secret" of Fatima. The person who incorrectly quoted me attacked me with some cutting remarks and criticisms, and then refused me the right to respond.* It took me a long time to straighten out all this nonsense. It is impossible to speak about Fatima without getting burned, and I cannot thank Renzo and Roberto Allegri enough for the way in which they tell this incredible story to the public without setting any fires other than that of the sun, the love and holiness that burned in the hearts of little Francisco and Jacinta.

Fr. Dos Santos Valinho, whom the authors have "challenged," has attempted to respond modestly without causing a sensation. He has affirmed that the famous secret refers to the Church, as Cardinal Ratzinger also asserts, and concerns the crises and divisions that have rocked it since the Council. He wisely does not say anything more.

Conscious of their specific mission as journalists, Renzo and Roberto Allegri left for Fatima with a professional concern to discover the unknown, but above all to understand life: what this prophecy is saying to men and women today in the context of contemporary history.

Starting with some solid documentation, the journalists followed up with various interviews on site in Fatima. The human and spiritual adventure of the three visionaries captivated them, fascinated them, and deeply moved them, and their testimony has given birth to a very interesting book that surpasses all expectations.

How and why?

As any good reporter would do, the authors met with those who were privileged to witness the events, such as João Marto, the ninety-four-year-old brother of Francisco and Jacinta. Still strong and lucid, he visited places from the past that are rich in memories from the time when he was ten years old.

Above all, though, Fr. José dos Santos Valinho—a Salesian priest who was born in Fatima and who is also Sr. Lucia's nephew and Francisco and Jacinta's distant cousin—won the hearts of Renzo and Roberto Allegri. The two journalists placed their trust in him, chose him as their guide, and recount a story that has the tone, the characteristics, the emotion, the beauty, and the intimacy of a story as told by a member of the family who is totally familiar with it. It is rich, therefore, with details that no other person could know.

This book has reached its goal. It is concrete, significant, sensitive, and penetrating. Renzo and Roberto Allegri have written it in a very professional manner, deeply aware of their specific task. They openly profess that they do not wish to compete with the historians, analysts, or researchers who are always on the lookout for unpublished documents; they simply want to relive the event in the same way that it continues to live in the hearts of eyewitnesses and pilgrims.

Besides, journalism and history are more closely related and more interdependent than it might seem. I venture to say this based on my own experience as a historian and journalist for *Le Figaro* after the Council. As a historian, I discovered that, beyond the dust of archives, historians terribly miss not having contact with the event itself and with its eyewitnesses, with the exception of contemporary historians, who are often considered the poor relatives of this discipline. Among other things, journalists have the difficult task of taking the first step to record the event in writing, a step that is alchemy before memory and history.

Many thanks, therefore, to Renzo and Roberto Allegri for having put their talent to the service of Fatima, the only shrine that two popes have visited three times, at a glorious and fervent time. These men open their hearts to the greater public, Christian and non-Christian, through this unusual, popular, and transcendent event that has never ceased to amaze the world and to influence the history of our times.

We are very grateful to the Virgin Mary for all this. She is the one who manifests women's primary and prophetic vocation forcefully yet discreetly in light of the Gospel, as do Elizabeth, the prophetess; Mary Magdalene, the first witness to the Resurrection, whom the apostles did not believe; and so many other figures. Mary is the one who was at the origin of Jesus' first miracle, the basis for the disciples' faith (see Jn 2:12). She is the one who was present at the main events in salvation history: the cruel death of her Son and the birth of the Church "in blood and water" (see Jn 19:25-27; Lk 1:41); Pentecost; and the first steps of a persecuted yet victorious Church.

Mary is the one who precedes the eschatological resurrection of the Church and all of humanity. In the same way, according to Revelation, chapter 12, Mary appears "in the sky, clothed with the sun and a crown of stars on her head," but also on earth joined with the Church, the mystical body of Christ, that very body that originated in her body at the time of the Annunciation. The Apocalypse is a manifestation of her solidarity with "the rest of her descendants" (Rv 12:17) where she is caught up in the unending spiritual battle (Jn 3:15) leading to the "last things" of salvation.

The Virgin of Fatima reawakens us to these forgotten values, to this future with God, of which we are such a priceless part.

René Laurentin

* After this interview—which was recorded in Fatima and broadcast by RAI 1—the press, apparently at a loss for news, released an exclusive news report that distorted my words and attributed to me a counter-reformist position: the secret of Fatima pitted against the Council. A journalist asked Cardinal Joseph Ratzinger in St. Peter's Square for his opinion on this interpretation. Another journalist interviewed Bishop Capovilla, who is a depository of the secret.

Both disapproved of Laurentin's opinion. The press published this reprimand. I sent in a clarification, saying that I had never made the statements for which I was reprimanded.

I presented my denial to Cardinal Ratzinger, and it also appeared in *La Croix* and in *Famiglia Cristiana*. He acknowledged that I was right. Bishop Capovilla even took the initiative to write me and tell me how displeased he was with the unjust way in which these rumors were circulated.

This is the reason why I say that it is dangerous at times to deal with Fatima. The news agency *Chrètiens-media*, which had published Ratzinger's so-called reprimand of Laurentin, repeatedly refused me the right to reply, in spite of the fact that such a reply had been agreed upon with Cardinal Ratzinger himself. Certain news agencies operate in such a manner, knowing well that Laurentin is too kind to sue them.

Introduction

Not a Fairy Tale

It all started at the beginning of the twentieth century, when Europe was on the verge of being swept up in World War I.

The new century had been heralded as the era of scientific progress, social evolution, and conquest. Humanity felt strong and powerful and was excited by each new achievement, often forgetting that every one of them was contingent on the right conditions. Among the affluent, a practical and ideological atheism was being propagated; among the poor, a desire for revenge was taking root, a revenge that materialistic socialism promised.

No one could have imagined, then, that the dawning century would turn out to be one of the most dramatic centuries in the history of humanity. It would be a century of great scientific, medical, and technological achievements, but also a century of bloodshed, inhumane cruelty, and horrendous suffering beyond all imagination: World War I; the tragedy of communistic totalitarianism in Russia and Eastern Europe, resulting in 150 deaths of innocent people; World War II with its concentration camps, bombings, and the Holocaust of the Jews, resulting in 56 million deaths; the atomic bomb, Hiroshima; Chernobyl; AIDS ...

At the time, no one could have foreseen these events. It was even impossible to imagine them. But one person was keeping watch, saw what was happening, and was worried. It was a very special person—a woman, a mother.

That person was Mary. She is the mother of Jesus, the Son of God who became man to redeem humanity. And she, the mother of Christ, also became mother of the entire human race.

It may seem like a fairy tale. But for a Christian, it is a dogma of faith—a truth that is more real and more solid than rock.

Faith tells us that Mary, our mother, continues to help the human race on its way. She is present, although mysteriously, in the life of every individual. But from time to time, when the need and the gravity of the situation require it, she chooses to help us in extraordinary ways, ways that are incomprehensible to our rational mentality but that become clear with time.

This is precisely what happened in Fatima, Portugal, in 1917, when the Virgin Mary appeared to three children—Lucia, Francisco, and Jacinta—who were ten, nine, and seven years old respectively at the time. She spoke to them about the destiny of the world. She gave them advice. And she entrusted some secrets to them. Some were revealed in time, but some are still unknown to us.

Mary predicted some events that seemed absurd at the time because they addressed realities that did not yet exist. Later, they all came true.

The story is not yet over. Two of the three children have now been beatified. They are Francisco and Jacinta, brother and sister, who died in 1919 and 1920 respectively. Lucia, who is still alive, was present at the ceremony. This event, which occurred on the eve of the third millennium of Christianity, has a prophetic significance that is related to a part of the secret that is still unknown to us.

A Decisive Meeting

Hundreds of books have been published about Fatima and the religious events that have made it famous throughout the world. The story of the apparitions, therefore, is well known in all its aspects. By writing another book, we do not make any pretense of adding anything new or of revealing something yet unknown.

However, as we visited that holy place in our capacity as reporters shortly after the news about the beatification of Francisco and Jacinta was announced, we had such an interesting experience that the idea occurred to us of writing a book so that others could "participate" in our visit.

While we were in Fatima, we met Fr. José dos Santos Valinho, a Salesian priest who is the nephew of Sr. Lucia, the only one of the three visionaries who is still alive. He guided us as we visited the places where the apparitions took place, and told us everything that happened in those places in 1917.

As he told us his stories, we noticed that he was not merely recounting the story as it has been widely reported: his account was filled with new and extremely interesting information. He included facts, anecdotes, words, and memories from his own experiences and from stories that had been told to him by his mother (Sr. Lucia's sister); his grandmother (Sr. Lucia's mother); Francisco and Jacinta's parents and siblings (who were also his relatives and whom he had known since childhood); as well as Sr. Lucia herself, his aunt, whom he continues to see and visit at least once a month. When he would say in his soft-spoken voice, "My aunt has told me," or, "My aunt has made it clear to me," our ears perked up with excitement because we immediately sensed that he was about to tell us something extremely important and valuable. These observations were coming from a primary source.

Fr. Valinho also introduced us to other people who had had an important role in these events, including João Marto, Francisco and Jacinta's brother, who is ninety-three years old but who still has a very clear mind. He too accompanied us to the places of the apparitions and to the homes where the three shepherd children were born and where they lived, telling us, "Here my grandmother used to … Here my mother would work, right there at that loom, while Lucia would …"

Everything took on an extraordinarily fascinating dimension when we were with Fr. Valinho; everything became more real and more genuine. Since he was Sr. Lucia's nephew, everything he said had the indisputable value of truth, which he had heard from the protagonists themselves. His account was free from the myths that encrust such events over time. We felt as though we were looking at a photo album with the person who had taken the pictures.

We went to Fatima searching for a news story, but we came back with more than enough material for a book. For this reason, we have decided to give a full and complete account of our trip. This book is, therefore, a report on a trip by two reporters who had the great fortune of getting to know some of the last surviving witnesses of the events at Fatima and of reliving through their stories the mystery that continues to interest and amaze the world.

Renzo and Roberto Allegri

1

AN INVALUABLE GUIDE

Reports about the beatification of Francisco and Jacinta Marto started to spread towards the end of June 1999. The Vatican confirmed these reports shortly thereafter with an official announcement: John Paul II had signed a decree authorizing the beatification of the two shepherd children of Fatima.

The announcement stirred up interest around the world. The media devoted space to the news, and those of us who are journalists were mobilized.

By announcing the beatification of Francisco and Jacinta, the Church was inviting people to reflect once again on the importance of the events that took place in Fatima back in 1917. Moreover, by scheduling it at the beginning of the third millennium during the Great Jubilee Year 2000, the Church undoubtedly wished to confirm that the events that took place there were still an integral part of history.

But the announcement of the beatification of the two Marto children immediately drew attention to another aspect, especially among the laity: the fact that Francisco and Jacinta were two little children. When they died, Francisco was eleven and Jacinta was nine.

The Making of Two Little Saints

Over the centuries the "glory of the altar" had become a privilege generally reserved for priests, monks, nuns, bishops, popes, and, to a much-limited extent, for laypeople, but always for people who were older. Now two little children had won this "glory." To be honest, other children had been beatified and canonized, but they were children who were martyrs, children whose fidelity to the faith cost them their lives.

For once the Church was applying the concept of sanctity to childhood. "The youngest people to be beatified in the history of the Church who did not die as martyrs," one news report heralded. People were fascinated by the news and were curious. We too were asking ourselves the same question that millions of others were asking when they heard the news: "Who were these two children?"

Until this point, everything about them had been related to the marvelous event in which they were involved. With news about their beatification, the spotlight was now focused on their lives. Everyone wondered how they had lived, what extraordinary things they had done besides having had the privilege of witnessing a heavenly apparition, how they had died, and what memories they had left behind about their short lives. If the Church had decided to elevate them to the glory of the altar and to hold them up to the world as models of holiness, they must have lived in some special way, and it would be interesting to know how.

This is what everyone was wondering at the time. And this is what we were wondering when we decided to go immediately to Portugal and do a report on the topic. We asked ourselves where could we get more information, and we thought of Fr. José dos Santos Valinho, Sr. Lucia's nephew, whom we had met while working on some other articles. We contacted him and left for Lisbon.

A Key Person

Portugal is a little European country on the Atlantic Ocean. Anyone who has visited it even one time cannot forget it. It is a land of sunshine and friendly people. It is a land of music.

Arriving in Lisbon by plane, we rented a car and headed north on the highway. Fatima is located seventy-five miles from the capital city, on the limestone plateau of the Estremadura.

On the same day, Fr. José dos Santos Valinho, who lives in Oporto, took a bus to Fatima. We were to meet each other at our hotel around three in the afternoon. But since he had arrived ahead of time, he left us a message saying that he would return around five.

Fr. Valinho is a Salesian priest who was seventy-three years old at the time we met. He was born and raised in Fatima and studied theology in Portugal and in Turin, Italy. He speaks Italian well. Given his "position" as Sr. Lucia's nephew, Fr. Valinho could be famous, known to and sought out by many. Instead, he is a quiet and humble person. He has never wanted to be in the spotlight, and he would never put himself in the spotlight. He agreed to help us out solely because of our friendship.

We were in the lobby of the hotel at 5:00 P.M. We knew that Fr. Valinho would be very punctual. We immediately spotted him walking to the hotel with a small cloth bag in his hand—the suitcase he uses for traveling—into which he had put only what was absolutely necessary for a few days away from home.

We walked up to meet him and exchanged cordial greetings. He is a very gentle and peaceful man. His face emanated goodness, simplicity, and optimism.

"Of course, you will be our guest at the hotel," we immediately told him. We invited him to check in so that he could rest for a while.

"No, no," he replied. "I'm going to stay with my sister. I've already called her, and she's expecting me."

He smiled and seemed relaxed. He had a warm glow in his eyes that is typical of people who are happy and at ease. He was very kind and gracious in his manner.

We were fully aware that we were very fortunate to have access to information from a person of Fr. Valinho's stature for our work. But now, seeing him and hearing him in person, we realized that his knowledge was even more important than we had thought. Fr. Valinho knows everything about Fatima; he is a key person for anyone who wants inside information on the marvelous story of Fatima from the source.

Time has inevitably left its mark on those distant events, often mythicizing them in a way that blurs them and empties them of their most beautiful and genuine content. But this is not the case with Fr. Valinho, who learned about them from many eyewitnesses and who continues to discuss them often to this day with his famous aunt, the sole surviving protagonist of these events.

The Visionary's Nephew

"What exactly is your relation to Sr. Lucia?" we asked as we sat down for a cold drink together in the hotel's little restaurant.

"I'm Sr. Lucia's nephew," Fr. Valinho said. "My mother, Maria dos Anjos, which means 'Mary of the Angels,' was Lucia's sister. She was her older sister. There's a fourteen-year difference between them. So my mother, in a certain way, was a 'second mother' for Lucia.

"They were very close. I remember going many times to visit Lucia with my mother. Usually they would reminisce. Lucia used to say, 'You even spanked me on many occasions because you didn't believe in the apparitions and wanted me to admit that I had made them all up.'

"'No, that's not true,' my mother would answer. 'It's true that I didn't believe you and I scolded you, but I never spanked you.'

"'Come on, now. You did too,' Lucia insisted. But my mother still denied it.

"It's very likely that she acted severely toward her little sister. But over the years, when what seemed quite impossible at the time turned out to be a very important event for the world, she never could believe that she had been so incredulous at the time. These were friendly discussions that showed how much the two sisters loved each other."

"What was Sr. Lucia's family like?"

"Besides my grandparents, Antonio and Maria Rosa dos Santos, there were six children: Maria dos Anjos, Teresa, Manuel, Gloria, Carolina, and Lucia—one boy and five girls. My mother was the oldest and Lucia was the youngest. Lucia was born five years after Carolina, so her brother and her sisters were already older when she began to walk and talk.

"She was the darling of the family. Often her brother and sisters would quarrel because they all wanted to carry her. My mother always said that Lucia was smart and very sweet. She was outgoing.

"She always wanted to express her affection physically. So whenever she came into the house after playing outside or tending the sheep, she used to hug and kiss her mother over and over again. This annoyed her sisters, and they used to call her 'the little hugger.'

"Lucia," Fr. Valinho continued, "endeared herself to everyone. My mother and my aunts, under the direction of my grandmother, spent their time weaving and making dresses. They didn't work in the fields. Since the neighbors had to go and work in the fields, they had my grandmother take care of their children. She became a sort of institution in the village: she knew how to read, she knew how to nurse the sick, and she was a good catechist. Therefore, my grandmother's house was like a day-care center for little children.

"My mother told me that all the children were incredibly fond of Lucia. Everyone was attracted to her. Everyone wanted to be next to her, to play with her, and to be held by her. All in all, she was an outgoing and happy child whom everyone liked."

"What is she like now?"

"She's old and her health isn't as good. Ninety-three years have taken their toll, and she suffers from rheumatism. But she still is happy and outgoing. She never complains and looks at everything philosophically and peacefully, manifesting a spirit of adaptability and adventure that keeps her young."

Memories of Lucia

"Do you visit her often?"

"Once or twice a month. I'm quite fortunate. She's a cloistered nun and can't have contact with the outside world. Moreover, there are explicit instructions that make her cloister even stricter. In fact, no one can visit Sr. Lucia unless that person has special permission from the Holy See.

"These instructions stipulate, however, that all her nieces and nephews who are directly related to her can visit her two or three times a year, while nieces and nephews who are indirectly related to her to the second or third degree can visit her only once a year. I, as a priest, can see her once a month and even more often than that."

"So you know her better than any other person?"

"We often visit together and chat about a lot of things, so I know her quite well."

"How did she react to news about Francisco and Jacinta's beatification?"

"With great joy. She has always been interested in the cause for the beatification of her two cousins. In her memoirs, which she wrote in the 1930s at the request of the bishop of Leiria, the Most Reverend José Alves Correira da Silva, she recounted everything she could remember about Francisco's and Jacinta's lives.

"For all practical purposes, no one knew them better than she did. When they went out to tend the sheep, they were together from morning until evening. During the time of the apparitions, she was the one who was responsible for their little group, the one who made the decisions, so the others confided in her. Even during the illnesses that led to Francisco's and Jacinta's deaths, she was the one who was their confidante and their comforter, the one in whom they confided their thoughts, feelings, and sufferings.

"Lucia is the primary source for being able to get to know Francisco and Jacinta. Her writings were instrumental in the cause for their beatification. This is why she was immensely happy upon hearing the news that everything turned out well."

"What did she say to you in this regard?"

"That she wanted to be present for the ceremony. Even when no one knew anything about the ceremony, she was convinced that it would take place in Fatima: 'It doesn't matter if we have to wait another year since the pope won't have time to come to Portugal during the Jubilee Year,' she said. 'But it would be wonderful if the ceremony took place in Fatima.'

"Then the news was announced that the beatification would be held in Rome on April 9, 2000. She told me, 'That's fine. I'm ready to go to Rome if the Pope permits me.'

"'But Aunt Lucia, you're already quite old and have many ailments. It's an exhausting trip,' I told her.

"'I don't plan to go to Rome on foot. There are planes that'll take me there. In Rome I'll find some monastery that will offer me hospitality, and then there are cars that can take me to the Vatican. If the pope invites me, then I'll go to Rome.'

"When she finally learned that the Holy Father had decided to come to Fatima instead, she was overjoyed and she repeatedly thanked the Lord for such a beautiful gift."

"How is she doing physically?"

"Her face is as smooth as a child's. Her eyes are sharp. But her legs aren't very strong, so she tires whenever she has to stand for a long time. Also, her hands are a little stiff and she gets tired when she writes. But nothing else bothers her. Let's hope that the Lord keeps her healthy for a long time."

Fr. Valinho looked at his watch.

"We should go," he said, getting up. "I've set up a first appointment for you with João Marto, Francisco and Jacinta's brother. He's waiting for us at his house. He's a rather extraordinary eyewitness. But it would be good not to keep him waiting."

2

FRANCISCO AND JACINTA,
MY BROTHER AND MY SISTER

We left the hotel and got into the car. Fatima is now a large town that has developed over the years around the shrine that was built on the site of the apparitions. The actual number of residents in the town is only eight thousand, but the number of beds reserved for tourists is well over ten thousand. There is a constant flux of pilgrims that amount to five million in a year.

We traveled down wide, shady streets lined with hotels, restaurants, and souvenir stores. At one point the street turned into an immense square that is twice the size of the square in front of St. Peter's in Rome. The shrine, with its distinctive tower that is 210 feet high, is located at one end. We stopped to take a look. Fr. Valinho prayed and then turned to us.

"When I was a boy," he said, "there wasn't even a house here, just land that was cultivated only in a few parts because most of it was too dry and rocky. Now everything has changed. But in Aljustrel, where we're going, things are different. There have been a lot of changes there too, but for the most part the village looks like it did back then."

Aljustrel, where the three visionaries Francisco, Jacinta, and Lucia were born, is a mile and a half from Fatima. We arrived there within a few minutes and found ourselves in a village where the houses—some old and some new—have kept their simple and modest appearance on the whole, as befits a little village in the country.

Fr. Valinho directed us to park the car in a large clearing. At one end there were some tables and benches under some trees. Probably they were there so pilgrims can stop and have something to eat on their trip.

"Wait here," Fr. Valinho said. "I'm going to see if João is ready to see you."

He got out of the car and went into one of the houses on the side of the clearing.

The Ninety-Year-Old João Marto

Thus our first stop was to visit João Marto, Francisco and Jacinta's brother. We had heard about him, but we had also heard that he has a hard time speaking with strangers, let alone journalists. He is very shy. Moreover, there was also a language barrier: João only speaks an old dialect that even the Portuguese have a hard time understanding.

Suddenly, Fr. Valinho's help turned out to be invaluable. He was born there and spent his childhood with João. He is perfectly familiar with the dialect that João speaks.

While we waited for Fr. Valinho to return, we reflected on how important it would be to hear João's testimony. Over time a whole myth has developed concerning Francisco and Jacinta, the protagonists in such an important event. Books and articles about them have altered memories, exalting their more exceptional characteristics and forgetting their more mundane side, which is so essential for knowing a person. But there is no way that João could have lost sight of these events.

He was two years older than Francisco and four years older than Jacinta. He was still a boy at the time of the apparitions. For children of that age, facts remain engraved in their memories with an indelible strength and precision.

Moreover, João, as Fr. Valinho pointed out, has always lived in Aljustrel and has always lived as a peasant. He has remained a simple man who has been unchanged by the fame surrounding his brother and sister. Thus he would be able to furnish us with some useful information for our research.

We caught sight of Fr. Valinho walking towards us, partially hidden by some bushes. He was with a very old man. They were walking slowly and chatting heartily. When they approached us, Fr. Valinho introduced us to the man who was with him.

"This is João Marto, Francisco and Jacinta's brother," he said, and the old man warmly extended his hand to us.

He was of medium height, with a face that had been baked by the sun and covered with numerous wrinkles that formed an intricate design. A pair of bushy eyebrows framed his attentive and inquiring eyes, which contained, perhaps, a touch of suspicion. He was wearing a cap that is typical of Portuguese peasants, a plaid shirt, and a heavy jacket. He was thrilled to be with Fr. Valinho, since the two of them are relatives.

"His mother, Olimpia, was married two times," Fr. Valinho explained. "Her first husband, José Fernandes Rosa, was the brother of my grandmother, Maria Rosa, the mother of my mother and of Lucia. There has always been a strong bond between our families, which was even more pronounced at the time of the apparitions. Do you remember, João, when I was a child? I was often at your house."

They conversed in their dialect, but it was impossible to understand them. João's voice was strong, precise, and clear. His sentences were concise and sharp. He certainly did not appear to be ninety-four years old.

We Were New Brothers

Fr. Valinho turned to us once again.

"There's twenty years difference between us," he said, "yet we went to school together. I was just a little boy, and he was already a man. My teacher wanted us to learn other subjects as well and encouraged us to go to a night school that she taught specially for adults.

"So I used to go to school during the day with the kids who were my age and at night with the adults. João was among them. Do you remember?"

João smiled and nodded in agreement.

Fr. Valinho asked him where he would like to sit for our conversation, and João said that he would prefer to be outside so he might breathe the evening air. He pointed to the benches under the trees.

There was no one there. It was a beautiful, cool day. It was about 6:30 in the evening, and the summer sun was setting with a subtle melancholy that penetrated the soul as the shadows slowly advanced.

Generally pilgrims head back to their hotels at this time of the day, or head to the shrine for evening services. The sky above was deep blue, almost dark. On the horizon the sun was a big, red ball, surrounded by vaporous clouds that are intense in color.

We walked over to the benches. João continued to converse with Fr. Valinho. If his brother, Francisco, had been alive, he might have been here with João, talking to us. He would have been ninety-two, and Jacinta would have been barely ninety-one.

We sat down. João sat with his hands on his knees. His hands were strong but marked by wrinkles and scars from working hard. We smiled at him and began to talk with him.

We directed our questions to Fr. Valinho, who translated both the questions and the answers. João seemed to be speaking very freely with us. He also agreed to have some pictures taken. But he did not show any emotion or enthusiasm.

"Have you always lived here?" we asked.

"Always," he answered, after Fr. Valinho translated our question. "I've always been a farmer and I've always worked the land here. The land here isn't very fertile; it's dry and rocky. But we manage. I live here with one of my daughters. I have a big family: four children—Laura, Maria, Francisco, and Jacinta—ten grandchildren, and six great-grandchildren."

When he spoke about his beloved family, his face glowed with pride. He smiled and looked at us.

"We used to play here with Francisco and Jacinta. We didn't have much time then to play. But on summer evenings, after having locked up the sheep, we gathered together here with the other children and played tag. Those houses weren't here back then. Our village was small."

"How many brothers and sisters did you have?"

"There were nine of us. My mother, Olimpia, had two sons with her first husband: Antonio and Manuel. Then she married Manuel Pedro Marto. José, Teresa, Florinda, and then another Teresa were born, followed by me, João, and then Francisco and Jacinta. There were a lot of us, but large families were normal back then."

An Overwhelming Passion

"What were your brother and sister, Francisco and Jacinta, like?"

"They were normal children, and there wasn't anything special about them. It didn't seem as if they had any special gifts. Francisco was a quiet guy and a little shy. He said very little, tended to daydream, and loved nature and animals. He could spend hours and hours alone, just looking at the countryside or watching the sunset.

"Jacinta, on the other hand, was very outgoing and a little capricious. She was the youngest in the family so she was pampered and spoiled. Consequently, she was naughty at times. But the things she did were normal things that all children do.

"Both Francisco and Jacinta liked music a lot. Francisco was very good at playing a wooden pipe that we used to make by hand from the branch of a plant that is like bamboo. They liked to sing, play, and dance."

"Dancing here in Aljustrel was very popular," Fr. Valinho interjected. "It was an overwhelming and irresistible passion. It was the main means of entertainment here in the country, and it involved everyone—young people, old people, and even little children.

"It was really an obsession. If someone started to play a few notes of a song, everyone would begin to dance. It's important to understand this to understand the people here.

"Even now you hear people say that certain children like to dance and sing. But it's different. The people here were born with this type of entertainment in their blood. It was second nature to them.

"During the different feasts that took place throughout the year, everyone danced. Even then there were special holidays during which these evening dances lasted two or three days in a row. My Aunt Lucia has often said that when she was a child she greatly enjoyed these dances.

"She has written about them in detail in her memoirs, probably to let people know that she wasn't any different from the other children and didn't spend all her time praying. She was really an outgoing little girl who liked to have fun. Nonetheless, God gave her so many blessings.

"My aunt," Fr. Valinho continued, "has told me many times that her sisters were the 'queens' of these holiday dances. Her mother insisted, however, that they take Lucia with them whenever they went to the dances. Then, so she would look good, her sisters dressed her very elegantly and put makeup on her just as they did on themselves.

"Lucia recalls that these dances took place during carnival time before Lent, as well as on the feasts of St. John, St. Anthony, and St. Peter—all the popular feast days. On the eve of these feasts, they built bonfires on the town square and danced next to the fires all night long. Then they would have dances at Christmas, on New Year's Eve, and on the special parish feast days such as the feast of the Sacred Heart and Our Lady of the Rosary. They also organized dances when they harvested the grapes and picked the olives.

"In addition, they used to have dances whenever someone got married. My grandmother, Lucia's mother, was very well known in this area, and she was always invited to the weddings that were held in Aljustrel and the neighboring villages, either as a godmother or as a cook. She used to take her daughters with her. On such occasions the dances began in the evening after the wedding banquet, and lasted into the night and even longer."

"She Was Crying and Dancing"

"My aunt told me that since she was so small her sisters used to put her on top of a trunk or a table during these dances so that she wouldn't be crushed by the people. There she sang, accompanied by an accordion or a guitar. She was already very good at dancing, and the people used to applaud her.

"My aunt told me that both Jacinta and Francisco were also extraordinary dancers. They especially liked to dance the *fandango* and the *vira*, two dances that were very popular back then. Jacinta, in particular, had a special passion for dancing. All that was needed was for some shepherd to begin playing an instrument, and she would start dancing—even by herself.

"To help me understand how much Jacinta liked dancing, Sr. Lucia told me a very beautiful story. One day Jacinta was crying because one of her brothers had gone off to the war and the family thought he had died in combat. To distract her, my aunt, along with two of Jacinta's brothers, began to dance. Immediately the little girl joined them, but she danced and cried at the same time."

Fr. Valinho continued his story, drawing on his vivid memories:

"Referring to the time in August of 1917 when, on the eve of the fourth apparition, they were locked up in jail, my aunt told me something particularly significant. She told me that they were in a big room, together with other prisoners. The three of them were crying, and the prisoners tried to console them.

"Then the children gathered together in the corner to pray the rosary, and the prisoners joined with them in praying. Some of them knelt down just as the children did. When they finished praying, the prisoners, in order to distract them, began to sing while one of them played the accordion.

"Jacinta, carried away by her love of music, began to dance. She was crying and dancing. Then one of the prisoners, a thief, started dancing with her.

"My aunt remembers that even in 1918, a year after the apparitions, Jacinta would get carried away by her passion for dancing. In spite of the important spiritual experiences that had deeply affected her life, she couldn't resist her passion for dancing. That year as carnival time was approaching, the boys and girls got together to organize a party.

"As usual, they decided to meet together at a particular house. Each person brought some oil, flour, and meat from home. The girls prepared a lavish banquet that everyone ate, then they danced into the evening."

"The World Started to Smile at Me"

"That year they were also going to invite Lucia so that she would be in charge of the festivities. At first Lucia refused. But then she gave in.

"She went with some friends to see the house where the party would be held. It had a beautiful room for dancing and a magnificent courtyard where the dinner could be held. She was all excited when she returned home, but she told me that her conscience was bothering her.

"She told Francisco and Jacinta about what had happened, and they scolded her: 'Are you going back to those dinners and parties? Have you already forgotten that we promised not to do that anymore?'"

Interrupting the account of the story, Fr. Valinho commented:

"It's worth stopping here and reflecting. Francisco and Jacinta, although younger, were already more spiritually mature than Lucia. Since they would be dying soon, they probably received more intense inspirations that were preparing them for heaven."

Then he continued his story:

"Hearing her two cousins' observations, Lucia tried to excuse her behavior by saying that everyone came to get her. How could she say no? It was Francisco who told her what she should have done.

"He said, 'Everyone knows that the Blessed Virgin appeared to you. So, you tell them that you've promised not to go dancing anymore and it's for this reason that you won't go. Then, when the day comes, we'll go to our hiding place in the country where no one will find us.' Lucia did what Francisco suggested, and when her friends heard about her decision, they decided not to organize the party.

"In her memoirs," Fr. Valinho concluded, "my aunt wrote that at that time 'vanity was my worst vice. In all honesty, the world started to smile at me, and especially my passion for dancing was beginning to root itself deeply in my poor heart. And I have to confess that if the good Lord did not show me his special mercy, the devil could have led me to damnation.'"

The whole time that Fr. Valinho was talking, João remained silent, nodding his head in agreement and smiling. Fr. Valinho gently took his hand.

"Forgive me for interrupting João's recollections," he said, "but I wanted to clarify this story about the dance, which is very important. Lucia, Francisco, and Jacinta were really normal, happy, carefree children before the apparitions, just as João said a while ago.

"When your brother and sister said that they had seen the Virgin Mary, how did people at home react?" I asked João.

"No one believed them. We thought it was impossible and that Francisco, Jacinta, and Lucia had invented the whole story. But their behavior completely changed.

"They prayed, made sacrifices, were always thinking about 'that woman' and talking about her constantly. They were a lot more peaceful and were always submissive. They didn't get angry, and if we teased them and were mean to them, they just smiled and accepted it without trying to get back."

In Father's Arms

"I was especially struck by Francisco, who began to pray almost constantly. Jacinta told me that the Virgin Mary, after having told Francisco that he was going to die soon just as she would, recommended that he pray many rosaries so that he would be worthy of heaven. Francisco always had his rosary in his hand so he could pray.

"He used to hide in the bushes and pray. Sometimes we looked for him, and when we found him, he looked as if he were daydreaming or were in a trance. We tapped him and pushed him to wake him up. My mother used to scold him because she had been looking for him for hours, and he used to answer, 'But I was always here. I was thinking about the Lord. I like to think about him, and I want to console him.'

"I didn't like to see him act like that. Sometimes I thought that he was suffering from some terrible disease or was under some kind of spell. Our parents were concerned, but not excessively.

"On the other hand, I saw that Aunt Maria Rosa, Lucia's mother, got very angry with her daughter. She used to spank her to try to get her to say that she had invented the whole story. Our parents were more understanding. Although they didn't believe them, they didn't scold my brother and sister."

"It's true. My grandmother was very worried," Fr. Valinho interjected. "She was a very religious woman and taught her children to be truthful above all. She wouldn't let them get away with lying, and for this reason she didn't feel peaceful when she heard Lucia talking about such sensitive things. 'I would have to be the one to suffer such a disgrace,' she said over and over.

"My grandfather, on the other hand, was more gentle and more understanding. Aunt Lucia has told me that sometimes when arguments broke out in the family, her father used to take her in his arms and carry her outside to the fields next to the house. He held her close to him, without saying a word, so that she would know that he loved her dearly. Perhaps he didn't believe her, but his behavior was more like that of Francisco and Jacinta's parents.

"On the other hand, my grandmother never felt peaceful. She felt betrayed, felt as if she failed in raising her daughter, and was worried about what other people were going to say. For her it was an awful tragedy."

The Frightening Crowds

"And you, João, when did you begin to believe that the Virgin Mary's apparitions might be genuine?" we asked, turning our attention once again to Francisco and Jacinta's brother.

"Much afterwards. More precisely it was when my brother and sister got sick. I realized that everything they said at home during the time of the apparitions was happening just as they said. At that point I knew that something extraordinary was happening.

"Several people from Aljustrel who were skeptical changed their attitude after the famous 'miracle of the sun' on October 13, 1917. But I wasn't there, so the miracle didn't make me change my opinion. I remember that my mother went that day to Cova da Iria, where the apparitions were taking place. She always went with Lucia's mother.

"The two of them were worried because an immense crowd had gathered at Cova da Iria. For some time Lucia had been saying that the Virgin Mary would perform a miracle on October 13, so curious spectators from all over Portugal and even from abroad were there. There were people from everywhere.

"The newspapers reported that there were more than seventy thousand people there. My mother was afraid that, in the end, the crowd would be furious because the miracle they were expecting wouldn't happen, and that the people would turn against the children and harm them. She hid at a distance, but was close enough to intervene quickly if she needed to.

"I didn't go," João repeated, "and I didn't see anything. I heard right away about what did happen since everyone was talking about it. It had rained all night long, and it was still raining in the morning. The people's clothes were soaking and all muddy since Cova da Iria was in an open field. It was still raining when Lucia, Francisco, and Jacinta arrived and started to pray the rosary.

"At a certain point, Lucia said, 'Look at the sun.' At that very instant the clouds broke and the sun appeared. But the sun wasn't still in the sky; it was moving, dancing, and whirling around, and it would come down from the sky as if it were going to fall on the crowd.

"The people who were there were afraid and were screaming. The phenomenon lasted a few minutes, then everything returned to normal. People realized that their clothes were completely dry. Even the newspapers wrote about this fact.

"The whole thing was unheard of, and many people who were skeptical at first believed. But I wasn't there and didn't see what happened, so I continued in the ranks of the skeptics. I remember very well that Jacinta and Francisco complained about this and told me that I was bad and that I would go to hell. But they would say it laughingly, and I didn't take them seriously.

"Then," João continued, "they both fell ill. During the second apparition, the Virgin Mary had already said that Francisco and Jacinta would die very soon, while Lucia would remain on this earth for a long time to bear witness to the apparitions. I thought this prophecy was just a joke.

"But when Francisco got sick and died in 1919, my skepticism began to waver. Shortly thereafter, Jacinta got sick. I remembered that she had often spoken about that illness.

"Aunt Lucia told me that one day Jacinta had asked her to come over in a hurry. She had told her that Our Lady had visited her there in that bed. 'Our Lady,' Jacinta had said, 'told me that I will be sent to two hospitals for treatment, but that I won't get better. It will just serve to make me suffer more for the conversion of sinners, and I'll die all alone.'

"Everything happened just as Jacinta said," João concluded. "She got pneumonia, and at that time such an illness was fatal. We tried to help her with every means possible at home, but it was useless.

"My parents cried, but she kept on saying that her time had come. They took her to the hospital of Vila Nova de Ourem, where she spent two months. They sent her home because there wasn't anything more they could do.

"Later on, friends and relatives convinced my parents to take her to a larger hospital in Lisbon to see if she would recover there. So they took her there, but the whole trip was pointless. She died on the evening of February 20, 1920.

"I thought a lot about what my brother and sister had said, and about the fact that it all turned out to be true. I realized at that point that something extraordinary must have really happened, and I began to change my mind about the whole thing."

The Sick Little Children

"Do you remember how your brother and sister acted when they were sick?"

"This is what I remember. They never complained, they weren't afraid of suffering, and they continued to pray and to offer their lives to God for the conversion of sinners. I believe they also saw apparitions. My mother remembers that when the end had come, Francisco looked at the window and said: 'Mama, look at the beautiful light.' He smiled as if he recognized someone he knew.

"On the other hand, Jacinta's illness lasted fifteen months. Jacinta suffered a lot but didn't show it. She repeated over and over to Lucia, who came to our house to visit her every day: 'I don't want you to tell anyone that I am suffering, not even mother, because I don't want them to be worried.'

"When her suffering was particularly great, she said over and over: 'O Jesus, now I can convert many sinners because this sacrifice is very great.' In short, they experienced joy in the midst of sickness and suffering, and this wasn't a normal thing."

"Did you think your little brother and sister would one day become saints?"

"Absolutely not."

"And are you happy now?"

"Of course, but I'm also worried. I think about myself and that I should be a better person and pray more. A while back I was invited to a conference in Lisbon that was organized by some priests. They asked me to say something about my brother and sister, and I told them what I remember.

"At the end of my talk, I expressed my concerns. I told them that if Francisco, who was so good and so innocent, had to say so many rosaries in order to go to heaven, what would I, a sinner, have to do? And what would they have to do? My words were followed by deep silence."

"Do you go to visit Sr. Lucia?"

"I go there from time to time. She always is happy to see me. We often tended sheep in the pasture together from the time when we were little. But since she was closer to my brother and sister, at a certain point I let them go with her."

"I've accompanied João to visit Sr. Lucia," Fr. Valinho said. "When they get together, they recall old times and it's a pleasure to listen to them. Every time I learn something new.

"One day I also accompanied João's parents, Manuel and Olimpia, on a visit to Lucia's house. I remember that my aunt told them, 'Now that your children are grown up and settled down, you can leave the world and enter religious life so that you can think only about matters of the soul. Aunt Olimpia can come here to the Carmelites with me. And you, Uncle Manuel, you can go to a Carmelite monastery.'

"My uncle was silent for a moment, then turned to Lucia and answered, 'For me that would be fine, but you have to realize that it would cause problems for your aunt. She's too attached to the world.'"

Fr. Valinho translated the anecdote for João, who was amused and laughed. Then he got up. It was already quite late. Saying goodbye, we noticed that João had three little badges in the buttonhole of his jacket. We asked him what they represented. He proudly showed them to us.

"This is the Italian flag. Some Italian pilgrims gave it to me, and I wear it because I like its beautiful colors. This one is the badge of an organization called 'Friends of Fatima.' They gave it to me when they made me an honorary member. And this one is the badge of another organization, 'Children of God.' They're souvenirs of people who have come to visit me."

We warmly shook his hand, and he walked toward his house.

"I'll accompany him, and then I'll go to my sister's house which is nearby," Fr. Valinho said. "We'll get together tomorrow morning. Come and get me around nine o'clock."

"You're not coming to dinner with us?"

"No, thank you. My sister's expecting me. Have a good evening."

"You, too, Father. We'll see you tomorrow morning at nine. We'll be on time."

Fr. Valinho helped João Marto, and the two walked off chatting with each other. They could easily have passed for two shepherds who were on their way home after a day's work. We stood there looking at them. From time to time João turned around and waved at us.

3

THE FRAGRANCE OF TIME

"There's not one place here that doesn't remind me of the three visionaries," Fr. Valinho said as he looked around.

He was standing on the doorstep of his sister's home, where he had spent the night. His sister's name is Maria Rosa, after her grandmother. We had met him at nine o'clock exactly, as we had agreed.

"That house," he said as he pointed to an old building on the other side of the street, "is Lucia's house, with a courtyard where my mother and my aunts organized parties and dances. Those old fig trees that you can see in the courtyard behind the house are the same ones that were growing there back then. Lucia used to hide behind them and play with Francisco, Jacinta, and other friends their age.

"The famous family well is located behind them, an important place for the visionaries. There they had some visions. They chose that well as a refuge, as a place where they could have secret meetings together, so that they could share their problems with each other and pray together when they were going through difficult times."

When Fr. Valinho turned around, his face was ecstatic. He seemed to be reliving some of those past events.

"I, too, spent part of my childhood in these places," he said. "Many times I heard my grandmother tell people about everything that happened to the visionaries. Francisco and Jacinta were already dead, Lucia had gone off to the convent, and my other aunts and uncles were married. But my grandmother continued to live here and tell people the story.

"I listened, but I was a little distracted. Being a little boy, I had other interests. Nonetheless, those events remained engraved in my memory, and when I suddenly began to understand the importance of those events, they became vivid in my mind. My mother never forgot those times and what happened back then. These places, these trees, and these walls are witnesses to many extraordinary events."

A Very Little House

We crossed the street. The house where Lucia was born has been carefully preserved and is now a museum that is administered by the shrine in Fatima. It is a simple, one-floor structure. Inside the rooms are small and are furnished with furniture and other items that belonged to the dos Santos family. Old photographs adorn the walls.

A woman was dusting quietly and discreetly. She was old and dressed as a peasant. Fr. Valinho introduced us to her.

"This is my older sister. Her name is Maria dos Anjos, just like our mother," he said. "She is responsible for maintaining Lucia's house. Visitors come every day, so everything has to be in its place. My sister cares for it with much love."

The woman smiled and continued working.

We visited the house. In each of the little rooms we were surrounded by silence and we felt a sense of awe. The various objects recalled a now-distant past and a different lifestyle. They seemed to belong to some fantasy world.

Suddenly we realized that the house must have been small for Lucia's large family of eight people. Fr. Valinho sensed this and said to us with a smile:

"Back in those times, all the houses were more or less this size and all the families were large. Space was limited, but people adapted. In a certain way it helped keep families more united. The bedrooms were usually reserved for the parents, while the children had their beds in other parts of the house.

"That's the loom that my mother used," Fr. Valinho explained. "My grandparents didn't have much land, and the little that they had was dry and produced very little. Therefore, while my grandfather and my uncle worked in the fields, my five aunts worked at home.

"My grandmother organized a weaving and dressmaking work-shop, and it grew to be quite large. Girls from quite a distance came to study here. My mother worked at the loom, while her sisters, Teresa and Gloria, sewed. Carolina and Lucia would help them out.

"At certain times of the year, even the women had to go work in the fields, so at those times they hurriedly did their sewing in the evening. My Aunt Lucia has often told me that during those times the whole family would gather and give the women a hand. Her father, for example, would fill the spools, and Uncle Manuel would play the accordion so that the hard work would seem lighter."

A Shepherd at the Age of Seven

"The children were in charge of taking the sheep to pasture. They started to do this when they turned seven, and would continue to do so until they were about thirteen. At that age they would turn the job over to a younger brother or sister, and the boys would start to work in the fields and the girls would begin to weave and sew.

"Children under the age of seven would stay at home, but they, too, helped with chores around the house. Lucia became a shepherd at the age of seven. Before her, the job belonged to Carolina.

"One day my grandmother said that Carolina had reached the age where she could now start working at home, and that Lucia would now be in charge of the sheep. My grandfather did not feel the same way, nor did Lucia's sisters. Lucia was the youngest child and everyone spoiled her, so no one in the family wanted her to have to work, even if it was small. But my grandmother said that Lucia was just like the other girls and there was no reason to make an exception for her. She was seven years old, so she had to start tending the sheep."

"What did Lucia do before this time?"

"Baby-sitting. She took care of the little children from the village whose mothers entrusted them to my grandmother's care while they went to work in the fields. You see, this was a very special situation. My grandmother was extraordinary. She was well educated and knew how to read, so the whole village held her in high esteem. All the people in Aljustrel knew her.

"She also knew how to nurse the sick. Whenever someone was sick, they came to her. She often visited the sick at their homes. If the sick person was a mother with small children, she used to bring the children to her house so that their mother could recuperate. Other mothers, who were forced to work in the fields, asked my grandmother to take care of their little children, so Lucia was in charge of them."

"Did she do so voluntarily?"

"Yes, very much so. And even the children realized it. They always wanted to be with Lucia and play with her. She was very good at organizing games.

"My grandmother often said to her, 'I don't know what kind of magic touch you have, but the children run to you like they would to a party.' For this reason, her cousins, Francisco and Jacinta, who lived in another part of the village, always used to come here to be with her. They practically grew up in this house.

"My Aunt Lucia has told me that Jacinta didn't always have a good attitude. She was very touchy. She always wanted to be the winner, and when she would lose, she would sulk. But my aunt has also told me that she was very sweet, lovable, tender, and charming."

"What kind of games did they play?"

"Games that children used to play back then: games with pebbles and buttons, guessing games, passing the ring, and taking aim. They also played cards, especially *briscola*, which was Francisco's favorite game.

"Jacinta, on the other hand, liked to play a certain game with buttons, which always caused problems. Whenever the players used up all their buttons and were losing, they used to pull the buttons off their clothing so they could keep on playing. Lucia always seemed to be losing. When her mother called her for dinner, she used to hurriedly sew the buttons back on her dress to avoid a scolding.

"My aunt has often told me that, besides having a little problem with getting angry quite easily, Jacinta also had a little problem with being stingy. She never wanted to give up the buttons that she won. In order to get them back, Lucia had to argue with her and threaten never to play with her again."

The "Angels' Lamps"

"Having heard my Aunt Lucia's stories, I was able to get a rather good idea of Jacinta's and Francisco's personalities. They were normal children, as João has said, so they had their strengths and their weaknesses.

"My aunt has said that Francisco did not seem at all like Jacinta's brother except for his features. He wasn't capricious and outgoing like she was. On the contrary, he was quiet and docile.

"When he played games, he seemed always to lose. If he did win but his opponent refused to concede him the victory, he gave in without putting up a fight and simply said, 'You think you won? Fine! I don't care!' If someone stole something from him, he simply said, 'Do what you want. Why should I care?'

"Sometimes Lucia used to take him by the hand, make him sit down on the ground or on a rock, and tell him to stay there quietly. He obeyed. He was well behaved and submissive, just the opposite of Jacinta, who was fiery, independent, and unyielding. But she, too, was very sensitive. She also was a daydreamer and had a lively imagination."

"What does Sr. Lucia still remember about Jacinta's personality?"

"Jacinta loved to look at the sunset and the stars in the sky. One of her favorite pastimes was to sit on the threshing floor in front of the house so she could look at the stars and sing to them. She called them 'angels' lamps,' because the moon for her was the 'Virgin Mary's lamp' and the sun was 'Jesus' lamp.'

"Both Francisco and Jacinta used these terms. They used them constantly when they were talking. Jacinta used to say: 'I prefer the Virgin Mary's lamp because it doesn't burn you and it doesn't blind you.'

"However, Francisco preferred the sun. 'No lamp is as beautiful as the Lord's,' he used to say. He loved to watch the rising and the setting of the sun. He was fascinated by the sun's rays that sparkled like a multitude of stars when they were reflected by windows or by drops of water on the trees."

"You've told us that Lucia's cousins and the children she cared for at her grandmother's house were fascinated by her. Were adults also fascinated by her?"

"Of course. Everyone in the village knew Lucia. She was the 'little princess.' Maybe it was because her sisters used to take her to parties and she was always well-dressed, and because she knew how to sing and dance.

"But it was especially due to the fact that she was a well-behaved, intelligent, and educated child who was very likable. When news got out around the village that Lucia had begun to take the sheep out to pasture, all the other shepherds, even those who were older than she, offered to go with her. This little detail shows how popular and how well-liked she was."

"Where did the children go to tend the sheep?"

"Around here. They didn't go far from home—only a mile at the most. They stayed on the family's property or in the forest, which was open to everyone. Lucia spent most of her time in those hills that are in front of us or at Cova da Iria, where the apparitions of the Virgin Mary took place on a piece of land that belonged to my grandparents."

"What was life like with the sheep?"

"A shepherd's life began very early in the morning. He had a big breakfast and then went out with the sheep. If he met up with other little shepherds, they decided together where they would go.

"They spent the whole day until sunset tending the sheep and playing together. They took a lunch with them, which consisted of some bread and cheese that they supplemented with some fruit from the forest and some edible herbs. Often they prayed the rosary together after their midday meal—especially the girls."

They Always Wanted to Be Together

"In this area it's always hot in summer, so people made some changes in their routines. It was impossible to work in the fields under the midday sun. So people began their work earlier, even at four in the morning, took a break around ten, and then started working again after four o'clock in the afternoon.

"The afternoon break was called a *siesta*. People spent the *siesta* at home or under a tree in the shade. Even the shepherd children adopted this custom. The sheep were taken to their pen for the afternoon and taken back to the fields for the evening. But the children never rested and took advantage of the *siesta* to play. Lucia, Francisco, and Jacinta usually played around the well, which was shaded by some huge trees."

"When did Lucia begin taking care of the sheep?"

"It was at the end of 1914. At the time, Jacinta was a little over four, and Francisco was six. They were both too little to be shepherds. João, who was eight years old and had his own friends, used to take the sheep out to pasture.

"Lucia turned down requests from all those who wanted to accompany her, and chose three friends who were her age. But Francisco and Jacinta couldn't bear having to spend the entire day away from her. Every morning they woke up early so they could see her. They used to meet her and play with her during the afternoon when she came back."

"When did Francisco and Jacinta begin to work as shepherds?"

"In 1916. They regularly asked their mother for permission to go with Lucia, but Aunt Olimpia would not budge. They finally managed to convince her when Francisco turned eight and could take care of his sister."

"What did Lucia, Francisco, and Jacinta look like back then?"

"There are some photographs of them together that were taken in 1916. From the expressions on their faces, it's clear that they were shy and embarrassed, at least in front of the photographer. But their faces and their eyes look like those of children who are vivacious, attentive, sharp, and clever.

"If you want to find detailed descriptions of what they were like and the impression they made, you have to wait until 1917 after the apparitions. You can find them in the newspapers and in the official documents of those who interviewed them.

"In one of these documents, Lucia was described as having 'a tall and wide forehead, large and lively brown eyes, narrow eyebrows, a pointed nose, a large mouth with big lips, a round chin, a head that was a little bigger than normal, and fine, blond hair. She is short and has a serious and innocent look. She is vivacious, intelligent, and friendly.'"

"What did they say about the other visionaries?"

"Dr. Carlos Mendes wrote about Francisco: 'With a beret perched on his head, a very short jacket, a vest that revealed a little of his shirt, and tight pants, he looked like a grown man in miniature. A fine young boy! He has a lively and mischievous look.'

"But Jacinta drew the most attention since she was so small. Everyone liked her. Dr. Formigão, the canon lawyer who was asked by church authorities to follow the events, described her in these terms: 'She is a little tall for her age, small-boned but not overly thin, with a well-proportioned face, dark complexion, and modestly dressed. Her skirt comes down to her ankles, and her appearance is that of a very healthy child, and she appears to be perfectly normal both physically and morally.'

"But the most precise portrait of Jacinta," Fr. Valinho concluded after a moment of reflection, "is found in a letter written by Dr. Carlos de Azaveda. He was a brilliant young man who followed the events in Fatima very closely. One day, after meeting Jacinta, he wrote his fiancée a letter describing how he felt when he met the little girl.

"Carlos de Azeveda's letter is very long and beautiful. I want to read you the most interesting parts. Let's go see my sister at work. There's a book there with the entire letter."

Very Shy

Once again we crossed the street to the little store that Fr. Valinho's sister had next door to the house. He looked through the books that were on sale there. He picked up one of them and slowly turned the pages looking for the letter.

"Here it is. Listen to what Carlos de Azeveda wrote to his fiancée after visiting Jacinta:

She is a very small and very reserved child. She approached me ever so slowly. I picked her up and sat her on a chest. I tell you, she's an angel.

She was wearing a scarf with a red design on it that was tied under her chin. The scarf was old and already worn. She also wore a little jacket that certainly wasn't her cleanest, and a long, red skirt that was very full, which is customary there.

I'd like to describe her face to you, but I don't think I would succeed in telling you anything that would approximately fit the description. The way in which she wore her scarf emphasized her facial features. Her eyes were dark and had an enchanting vivaciousness to them. Her expression was angelic and had a charming goodness to it.

Overall she was an extraordinary person who attracted you, but I don't know why. She was very shy. It was difficult to get her to say a few words in response to my questions.

After talking and (don't laugh) joking with her for a while, Francisco arrived. Jacinta began to warm up to us. After a while, Lucia also arrived. You cannot imagine Jacinta's joy when she saw her. She ran up to her and wouldn't let go of her.

"This is a portrait that depicts the true and authentic grace of this child, who really was an angel."

"Is the house where Francisco and Jacinta were born far from here?"

"No, it's behind those houses that are there in front of us. Francisco and Jacinta's nephew oversees the house, and last night I told him that we would visit him. Undoubtedly he's there waiting for us."

We walked down the street toward the main street, through Aljustrel. Pilgrims were already walking around. Four large buses were parked in an open space, and a group of French pilgrims was getting out.

The house where Francisco and Jacinta were born faces the street, nestled between some new buildings. It has been preserved as it was at the beginning of the twentieth century.

Fr. Valinho pointed to a date that is engraved over the entrance: 1897.

"That's the year in which Manuel Marto married Olimpia. This house was part of her dowry. It was built for them. Their children were born in this house."

We went in, and an elderly gentleman in his seventies walked up to meet us. His name was Giovanni. He is Francisco and Jacinta's nephew, who is in charge of the house.

Giovanni spends his days inside the house, serving visitors. He meets people of every nationality and has learned phrases in various languages. He even speaks a little Italian. He told us right away that the number of pilgrims was regularly increasing. Since the announcement of the beatification, the number of pilgrims had doubled.

The house is also very little. It is hard to believe that eleven people lived here, the number of people in the Marto family after Jacinta's birth, who was the last child. There are only a few rooms, all with dirt floors. In the bedrooms are the two beds where Francisco and Jacinta lay when they were sick.

"Did both of them die here in this house?" we asked.

"Francisco died in that bed," Fr. Valinho said. "He died on the morning of April 4, 1919. Jacinta was already sick. She lived for another year. She was on that other bed, but towards the end, when her condition was very serious, they took her to a hospital for treatment. She went first to the hospital in Ourem, and then to Dona Stefania Hospital in Lisbon, where she died all alone on February 20, 1920."

Her Body Was Intact

Some photographs that have turned yellow from age were hanging on the wall. In one of them, you could clearly see Jacinta, who was dead.

"That picture was taken on September 12, 1935," Fr. Valinho explained. "That day Jacinta's mortal remains were transferred from the cemetery of Vila Nova de Ourem to the one in Fatima. The casket was opened for identification, and, despite the fact that fifteen years had passed since her death, Jacinta's body had remained intact.

"Various pictures were taken, and the bishop of Leiria, the Most Reverend Alves Correira da Silva, sent some of them to Sr. Lucia, who was in Pontevedra, Spain, at the time, a nun in the Congregation of St. Dorothy. On November 17 of that year, Lucia wrote to the bishop to thank him:

> Thank you very much for the pictures. I can't tell you how grateful I am, especially for the one of Jacinta. I wanted to pull off the cloth that was covering her so that I could see her in entirety. I impatiently tried to uncover the face of her body, until I realized that it was a picture and not really her face.
>
> I was beside myself with joy at seeing my dearest childhood

friend. She was a child only in age. In other areas of her life, she knew how to practice virtue and demonstrate her love for God and the Virgin Mary through sacrifice.

I asked Giovanni, the caretaker, if any of the pilgrims who visit the house ever say that they have received any special graces through the intercession of the two children. Giovanni smiled. He opened a drawer in an old table and showed us a stack of letters.

"I keep these," he said, "because they are all testimonies written by people who state that they have received miracles through the intercession of Francisco and Jacinta. Look. They send their pictures and medical certificates, and tell their stories. All these letters have arrived recently; I've already taken all the others to the shrine, to the office for the cause of their beatification. Many people have said that they have received extraordinary graces through Francisco and Jacinta's intercession."

As we have already noted, the beatification process requires the investigation and discussion of a miracle that can be attributed to the candidates after their death. This is the last juridical step in the process. We asked Fr. Valinho if this procedure had been observed for the two visionaries from Fatima.

"Certainly. It is the procedure that has been sanctioned for the cause of all saints, and it can't be ignored. Moreover, it's very important.

"The process of beatification has two phases. The first is an investigation that the Church carries out. It is actually the preliminary process. The behavior of the person is scrutinized for holiness, to see if the person has heroically demonstrated the gospel virtues. The purpose of the process of beatification is to investigate, verify, and demonstrate that this is the case."

A Difficult Process

"At the end of a long investigation that at times can last for years and years, the pope can solemnly proclaim that the candidate led a saintly life and that his or her life can serve as an example for the faithful to follow. But the Church does not want to risk making a mistake in such a delicate matter. Therefore, she seeks help from above.

"She asks God to give a sign that will confirm the results of the investigation. That is, she asks for a miracle that can be attributed to the intercession of the candidate. It's like a supernatural seal on the whole process, divine approval that reassures us that the right conclusions were reached.

"There are no exceptions to this rule, except in the case of martyrs, who have been put to death for their faith. In cases where people have given up their lives in order to remain faithful to God, miracles are not required. No one doubts that they immediately went to heaven because their witness is so heroic.

"But you have to remember," Fr. Valinho emphasized, "that verification of the miracle is made through another long and meticulous process that is divided into two parts. During the first part, a commission of medical experts, who aren't always believers, has to ascertain that the healing being investigated has 'no scientific explanation.' At this point a commission of theologians and cardinals study the case to see whether it really involves God's supernatural intervention and to establish whether the miracle can be attributed to the candidate. A miracle is proclaimed only if these two conditions are met, and the way is open then for beatification."

"So you know the person who was miraculously healed through the intercession of Francisco and Jacinta?"

"Yes, I know her. She's a woman named Maria Emilia Santos. She lives in Leiria. I've already contacted her and she's expecting us. Let's visit her."

4

A Double Miracle

We immediately headed to Leiria, the capital of the province where Fatima is located. It is about eighteen miles from Aljustrel. The road winds through a hilly area that is rich in vegetation.

During our trip, Fr. Valinho told us a little about Maria Emilia Santos, the woman whose healing has been recognized as a miracle obtained through Francisco and Jacinta Marto's intercession.

"She's very shy and doesn't like meeting strangers," Fr. Valinho warned. "She lives at the institute where she received care while she was sick. When the healing was proclaimed to be a miraculous healing by Church authorities, Emilia was literally besieged by journalists who wanted to hear her story.

"At first she spoke with all of them because she felt it was her duty to witness to the blessing she had received. But after reading some of their reports, she realized that some of her statements were distorted. She felt very hurt, and since then she has no longer wanted to speak with reporters. But when I told her that you came from Italy, she agreed to meet you."

Because of the road work that was in progress on the outskirts of Leiria, it took a long time to get to the center of town. St. Francis Institute, a nursing home for people who are chronically ill where Emilia still resides, is a big yellow building. We found it without any difficulty.

Twenty-Two Years in Bed

"It's twelve thirty," Fr. Valinho noted, looking at his watch. "It's probably best to see if she would like to visit with us now or if we should come back later in the afternoon."

We parked in front of the institute under some large trees near a little pond. Fr. Valinho walked up to the door while we waited under a willow tree. A curious cat saw us and approached us.

"Come in. Emilia is waiting for us."

Fr. Valinho's voice was full of joy. We joined him and went into the institute together.

The woman who had been healed was waiting for us in a little room reserved for guests. We smiled at her. She was an older woman who was very petite and looked as fragile as a little bird.

"These are my friends who are gathering information for a book about Francisco and Jacinta," Fr. Valinho said. "They would like to know about your sickness and your miraculous healing."

Emilia smiled. Her face glowed with happiness, and her eyes were beaming. Right away we saw that she was still very moved by the memory of this miracle.

"It's something that changed my whole life," she said in what seemed to be an effort to justify the strong emotions that she was unable to hide.

"We understand," Fr. Valinho observed.

"My healing took place on February 20, 1989, the anniversary of Jacinta's death," Emilia pointed out. Clearly she wished to emphasize the importance of this particular coincidence.

She smiled again and then began to tell her story. Contrary to her appearance, her voice was full of energy, although her emotion broke through from time to time.

"I was bedridden for twenty-two years. My backbone had calcified, and I couldn't even move. My legs were all stiff and contorted. They were completely turned around.

"They tried every remedy possible, and I spent eight years in the hospital. But finally they told me that there was no cure. For this reason, they brought me to this nursing home, which is reserved for people who are chronically ill.

"One day Fr. Antunes came to see me, a priest who works at the shrine in Fatima. He told me about some spiritual exercises they would be holding at the shrine, and he asked me if I wanted to attend.

" 'I'd love to,' I replied, 'but in my condition, how could I? I'm not even able to move.'

" 'Don't worry,' he said. 'We'll take you on a stretcher, and there will be someone there to help you, just as they do here.'

"So I went to Fatima for the spiritual exercises. The priest who preached the retreat mentioned Francisco and Jacinta over and over again, as well as the Virgin Mary's apparitions. Little by little I was convinced that maybe these two children would be able to help me. That is, they would be able to give me the grace to be healed."

"Get Up. You Can Do It."

"However, it seemed to me," Maria Emilia continued, "that it was too much for me to obtain such a healing. I was convinced that I was not worthy of it, so I began to pray. I asked Francisco and Jacinta to at least give me the grace to be able to sit up in bed so that I would be less work and less trouble for the people who were caring for me."

"Then what happened?" we asked inquisitively.

"I returned home still on a stretcher, and I kept on praying. After a while, my prayers were answered. One morning I realized I could move in my bed.

"It was wonderful and astonishing. After years and years of being stretched out without moving, I slowly began to bend my back so that I could be in a sitting position. It was so extraordinary that it seemed like a dream.

"I wasn't able to move anything else, and my legs still were contorted and numb. Just the same, it was a big and unexpected improvement. I was very happy.

"After my initial surprise and joy, however, I realized that I really hadn't obtained what was most dear to me, which was not to be a burden for those who cared for me. Even if I was able to sit up, they still had to wash me, change me, turn me, lift me, and move me, because I absolutely could not move on my own."

"At this point, what did you do?"

"I was like that for another two years. Then I began to pray again. I said to Jacinta and Francisco, 'You granted me the healing I requested, but not to the extent that I thought. I didn't want to be a burden for those caring for me, but even though I can sit up, I'm still dependent on other people for everything. Now I ask to be healed of everything so that I can take care of myself without the need for any assistance.'

"I felt deep down inside that Jacinta and Francisco would be able to grant me this second favor, too. By then I understood that I could truly obtain it by praying fervently and in faith. I began a novena. Then I did a second novena."

"Is that when the miracle occurred?"

"Yes. On the evening of February 20, 1989, I was in my bed and I was praying. I remembered that it was the anniversary of Jacinta's death that day. Sixty-nine years before, on February 20, she had gone to heaven while she was only a ten-year-old child.

"I was reflecting on this particular fact. I was deeply moved, and I intensified my prayer. At a certain point, I heard a voice within me say, 'Get up. Get up. You can do it.'

"I thought it was simply the power of suggestion. No one could be speaking to me in my room; I was all alone. But I heard the voice again, saying clearly and distinctly, 'Get up and walk. You can do it.' Then some mysterious power pushed me up from my bed."

For the Lord Nothing Is Impossible

"I felt an immense joy in my heart. My heart was beating rapidly. I thought it was going to pop out of my chest.

"I realized that, even though I had been thinking about a healing, I still was a little afraid that another miracle might be happening. I sat for a while on my bed without moving, listening to my feelings. Then I tried to move a leg and realized that I was able to do so. Then I tried moving my feet, and I realized that they were no longer bent unnaturally and that I could move them without difficulty.

"I was overcome with joy, and my heart was racing. I stayed under the covers for a while; I couldn't believe it. Then I tried to move once again. I was really able to do it! I got my courage up, and I decided to get up.

"I threw my legs off of the bed and put my feet on the ground. My legs were no longer numb. In fact, I was even able to feel the cold floor, which I hadn't been able to feel for years and years.

"I pushed myself with my arms, and I stood up. I was on my feet. I took a step, then another. Suddenly I felt tears running down my face because I realized that I was able to walk. Even my crooked spine had straightened out. I felt like I could move it, and I was able to bend over perfectly when I tried to do so.

"Quickly I began to walk out of my room. I walked in front of another patient, who saw me and immediately knew what had happened. She began to cry out. Some nurses came and saw that I was healed."

"What did you do?"

"I walked by myself to the director's office, who was already asleep. It was ten o'clock at night. I knocked on her door and told her that I could walk.

" 'Don't lie,' she answered.

" 'No, I'm walking, I'm walking,' I said over and over. 'Jacinta and Francisco have blessed me.'

"She got up and came to see for herself. She, too, was amazed. The next day some doctors, who had been caring for me for years, came to see me.

" 'Impossible,' they repeated over and over again while they examined me. 'No human power could have done such a thing.'

" 'That's right,' I answered. 'No human power could, but nothing is impossible for the Lord.'

"It's been ten years since that day, and I'm still fine and walk normally. I've never had any trouble with my back, feet, or legs. It's as if I had never been sick."

Maria Emilia could not hold back her tears. She got up and invited us to follow her to the garden. She walked very agilely, without limping. When we saw her, we could not imagine that she had been completely paralyzed in bed for twenty-two years.

We went outside to a small garden where there were some flowers. Maria Emilia agreed to pose for some pictures. Our meeting was over. We said goodbye, thanking her for kindly seeing us. Maria Emilia took our hands and hugged us. We felt as if we were bidding farewell to an old aunt whom we had not seen for a long time.

We were so happy with the meeting that, before heading to Fatima, we even greeted the cat that was now curled up waiting for us on the hood of our car.

5

The City Named
After a Princess

Our meeting with Maria Emilia Santos made a deep impression on us. As we sat in the car looking for the road to Fatima, we kept recalling everything she had told us and the disarming simplicity with which she spoke of the miracle.

"She must be an extremely good woman," we observed.

"She suffered for many years and accepted her condition without complaining," Fr. Valinho noted. "When suffering is lived out with such peace and strength, it becomes an extraordinary school of life."

Although we had circled around the institute and made our way to the main street in town, we were not sure that it was the same route we took when we arrived.

"Which way should we go now?" we asked Fr. Valinho.

Fr. Valinho glanced at the road map on his lap.

"To return to Fatima, we should go straight ahead, but it might be better to turn right. I want you to visit Batalha. It's not far from here. We'll have to go a little out of our way, but you can't come to Portugal without visiting it."

We turned right into a street full of traffic.

"Father, what is Batalha?"

"It is one of the most beautiful architectural monuments in the world. I'm surprised you haven't heard of it. Batalha, which means *battle* in Portuguese, is a church with a monastery attached to it that was constructed at the end of the fourteenth century.

"Both are dedicated to the Virgin Mary and demonstrate how Portugal has always had a deep devotion to the Mother of God. Here's the map. It's still another six miles from here."

An Amazing Wonder

Within minutes we were outside the city limits. There was less traffic. The road was smooth and wound its way through green fields.

"Around 1385," Fr. Valinho told us, "the kingdom of Portugal was going through one of the most serious crises in its history. King Ferdinand, the last ruler of the Borgogna dynasty, had died, and the heir to the throne was his only daughter, Beatriz, who had married the Spanish king, Juan of Castile. According to the laws of that time, Portugal should have been annexed to the dynasty of Castile, thereby losing its independence.

"But the Portuguese rebelled. They didn't want to become part of Spain. Therefore, the Spanish threatened to occupy the country by force.

"The Portuguese decided to defend themselves, but their army was rather pitiful compared to that of the enemy. So the chief commander, João d'Avis, who then became King João I (thereby beginning a new dynasty), made a vow to the Virgin Mary that he would build a huge church in her honor if he won the battle against the Spaniards."

"Did he?"

"Of course. The battle took place on August 14, 1385, near Aljubarrota, and the Portuguese were the victors. Two years later, construction was begun on the church, right near the place where the battle took place.

"King João I summoned the most famous architects from Portugal and from Europe to work on the project. The principal architect was Alfonso Domingues, who was Portuguese. He constructed a monastery, which was entrusted to the care of the Dominicans, as well as a large church. The whole complex was dedicated to the Virgin Mary and called Santa Maria della Vittoria di Batalha."

Before we knew it, we had arrived in the vicinity. The church loomed on the left and we were dumbfounded. Even looking at it from a distance, it appeared imposing, regal, and majestic. As we approached it, we realized that before us stood a unique architectural monument.

We parked near the church and walked to it in silence. Words cannot describe what we saw. It was built in the Gothic style, but it had been embellished with a whimsical elegance that is typically Portuguese. Fr. Valinho was very generous in giving us information. He showed us the rose window and the statues of the angels and the prophets at the entrance.

When we entered, we were so flabbergasted at the sight that we were literally at a loss for words. The light that glowed through the stained-glass windows illuminated three very tall marble naves and all the columns and statues. It is simply gorgeous. Nothing is more conducive to prayer than a Gothic building that rises up to the heavens. For a long time we stood still, immersed in total silence.

Unfortunately, our time was limited and our visit was rushed. But one thing is certain: we will never forget it. As we continued on our way, Fr. Valinho continued his explanation.

"The Virgin Mary has always had an important place in the history of Portugal. Ever since the time of its first king, this country has been called the 'Land of the Virgin Mary.' In 1646, King João IV, along with representatives from the clergy, nobility, and the common people—the three main social classes of the time—swore an oath of eternal fidelity to the Virgin Mary under the title of the Immaculate Conception.

"From that moment on, the Virgin Mary was proclaimed the queen and patron of Portugal. And from that moment on, no Portuguese queen ever wore a crown, since it was an emblem reserved exclusively for the Immaculate Virgin Mary.

"There are numerous shrines dedicated to the Virgin Mary in this country. The one in Batalha is certainly the most important and the most famous because of its artistic value and the fact that it is the tomb of the rulers of Portugal. But there are many other shrines, and they are all very beautiful."

Neither God nor Religion

When Fr. Valinho spoke about the history of Portugal, he did so with passion. He told us that in ancient times the country was a Roman province. Then it was invaded by the Moors and only regained its independence in 1138.

"Portugal," he said, "is a country of navigators and explorers, including the first ones to set out on the open seas searching for other inhabited lands."

Fr. Valinho explained that in the 1800s Portugal suffered from relentless decadence. Consequently, confusion and revolt flooded the 1900s. In 1908 King Carlos and his firstborn son, Felipe, were assassinated. Manuel, his second son, was overthrown by a military coup, which brought the Republicans to power.

"Those were difficult times," Fr. Valinho said. "The vast majority of the people, who were mainly peasants, were divided by opposing ideologies and ongoing revolutions, and tormented by extreme poverty. In fifteen years there were fifteen revolutions, and forty different governments followed one after another.

"Economic and social conditions were disastrous. Even in the religious sphere there was a sort of division. The masses of people were practicing Catholics, but the government and the intellectuals professed an atheistic and Masonic secularism.

"The old, traditional religiosity of the country's ruling class gave way to rulers who were intent on unleashing a war on the Church. In fact, in 1911 the head of state, Alfonso Costa, approved a law separating Church and state. Upon doing so, he triumphantly declared, 'Thanks to this law, Portugal will be able to completely eliminate Catholicism within two generations.' Children were forced to parade through the streets holding banners with the inscription, 'No God, No Religion.'

"It was amid this climate that the Virgin Mary arrived with her help," Fr. Valinho continued. "We might never know the reason for such a heavenly initiative or why the Virgin Mary chose Portugal, Fatima, and the three children from Aljustrel. But the help that Mary wanted to give certainly did not involve only this country: it involved the whole world.

"Undoubtedly Mary knew that the world was facing difficult times. She knew that men had constructed a history that was robbing them of the truth and leading them on the road to destruction. So she, who is a mother, wanted to intervene."

Mohammed's Daughter

"Is there really no reason that would help us understand why the Blessed Virgin appeared at Fatima in order to give her messages?" we asked.

"From what I know, there isn't," Fr. Valinho answered. "Fatima is a very ancient town. Given its location far from any city, the impact of the different crises of which I spoke was felt only minimally. It remained a little peasant village, which the authorities ignored.

"It was very dependent on the town of Vila Nova de Ourem, whose mayor, Artur de Oliveira Santos, was a proponent of the new political stream. He was an atheist, an anti-cleric, and a Mason, and he passionately hated anything connected with God and religion. He published a newspaper called *O Ouriense,* where he vented his spite for religion. He also founded a Masonic lodge over which he presided.

"But his ideas, which were also shared by some fanatic followers, never filtered down to the mass of peasants in the countryside, who remained faithful to the religion of their forefathers. Nonetheless, the hard and difficult times were taking their toll."

"Fatima is a Muslim name," we observed. "It was the name of one of Mohammed's daughters."

"That's right. You should know that during the time of the wars to free Portugal from Moorish rule around 1140, a violent battle was waged at the town of Alcacer do Sal, the capital of the province of Al-Kasar. While a group of Moorish men and women were having fun on the banks of the River Sado, they were attacked by a band of Christian cavalrymen who were led by Gonçalo Hermingues, a ferocious commander who led surprise attacks like a streak of lightning.

"The Christians massacred most of the people, but those who survived were taken as prisoners to Santarem, where they were entrusted to the king, Alfonso Henriques. The king asked the valiant Hermingues what reward he wanted, and the warrior asked for the hand of Fatima, the daughter of the Valì di Alcacer, whom he had taken as a prisoner. His wish was granted.

"Hermingues was so in love with Fatima that he left the army at her request. After his fiancée converted to Christianity and received the name of Oureana in baptism, he married her. The king gave the city of Abdegas to the newly married couple as a wedding gift. It was renamed Oureana in honor of the bride. Later it became known as Ourem.

"But the lovers' happiness was short-lived. Oureana died at a young age, and Hermingues, who could not be consoled, retired to a monastery. He buried the body of his beloved wife in a town east of Oureana, where a new monastery was being built, and gave it the original name of his wife, Fatima."

A Solid Religious Tradition

"At the beginning of the twentieth century," Fr. Valinho continued, "Fatima was practically unknown. Its inhabitants were very peaceful, simple, and happy peasants. As I already told you, they loved to party, and everyone—including the children—had a special passion for music and dancing.

"But they also were deeply religious, and their faith was as solid as a rock. My grandparents, who were Lucia's parents, as well as my aunt and uncle, the Martos, who were Francisco and Jacinta's parents, were families that were dedicated to observing all the laws of the Church. My Aunt Olimpia, who was Francisco and Jacinta's mother, told me that she could not recall missing a single Mass, even when her children were small.

"Like almost all the peasant families in Portugal, my grandparents, aunts, and uncles observed the custom of praying the rosary together in the evening. This helps us to understand the strength of their spiritual life.

"My grandmother, as I've said, was a pillar in the parish. She taught catechism to the children in the village of Aljustrel, and she taught them so well that the pastor of the parish had complete confidence in her. When he found out a child had learned his or her catechism from my grandmother, he would let that child receive the sacraments without any difficulty."

"Speaking of the sacraments, when did the three visionaries make their first Holy Communion?"

"Well, at that time children customarily made their first Holy Communion when they were ten years told. People felt that they only could grasp the importance of the sacrament they were receiving when they were that age. An exception was made, however, for Lucia. She made her first Holy Communion when she was only six years old."

"How did that happen?"

"It was because of the catechism lessons that her mother gave her. From the very moment that her mother began giving lessons at home, Lucia went to all of them, and by the age of six she knew the whole catechism by heart. My grandmother didn't dare ask the parish priest, Fr. Pena, to let Lucia make her first Holy Communion, because she knew that the rule was to wait until the age of ten. But she secretly hoped this would happen.

"When it came time for her daughter, Carolina, to go to the catechism classes that the priest gave for those children who would be receiving their first Communion, she also sent Lucia along with her sister. The priest realized that the little girl knew all her catechism. She sat right in front of him.

"When one of the students couldn't answer his question, he would ask Lucia if she knew the answer in order to embarrass the student. She knew the answer every time. When the course was over, he gathered all the children in the church to let them know who deserved to make their first Communion.

"He asked Lucia to come up and said, 'You know doctrine very well, but you have to wait until you're at least seven.' Lucia began to cry. Because of all the compliments she had received, she had gotten her hopes up, and now she was disappointed.

"At that very moment, a priest who had been called in to help with confession entered the church. His name was Fr. Francisco Cruz, a very learned and deeply respected Jesuit, whose cause for beatification is being studied. He asked why she was crying.

" 'The little girl knows her catechism very well,' the priest said. 'But she's only six, so I can't let her make her first Communion.'

" 'Let me quiz her,' Fr. Cruz replied. He took Lucia into the sacristy and, after a while, returned to the church.

" 'This child,' he announced, 'knows her catechism better than anyone, and knows perfectly well what to do.'

" 'But she's only six,' the priest repeated.

" 'That doesn't matter,' Fr. Cruz said. 'If you want, I'll take responsibility for her.'

" 'Very well,' the priest decided. He turned to Lucia. 'Go tell your mother that tomorrow you'll be making your first Communion.' "

"Lord, Make Me Holy"

"That day was a joyful day for the family. Lucia's sisters, especially my mother, who was the oldest, stayed awake all night making a white dress, veil, and train. In the morning they dressed little Lucia and then had her brother, Manuel, carry her in his arms to the church so that she wouldn't soil her white dress, which went down to her feet. Since she was the smallest in the group, she was put at the head of the line."

"Have you ever spoken to Sr. Lucia about this?"

"She has never forgotten that day. Every so often she'll talk to me about it. She said her heart was racing at the thought of receiving the consecrated host, and she remembers that when her mother came to get her to go to church, she told her, 'Above all, ask the Lord to make you holy.'

"Her words remained engraved in her mind. She has told me, 'Those are the first words that I told the Lord when I received him.' "

"What about Francisco and Jacinta?"

"They, on the other hand, weren't as fortunate. They made their first Communion after the Blessed Virgin's apparitions. Francisco literally made his first Communion on his deathbed. But since they spent so much time with Lucia, they heard her always speaking about Jesus with such a passion that they, too, fell in love with him as if he were someone they saw every day.

"I want to share with you a little episode that illustrates how the faith of these three children was a simple but living faith. Back in those days, the feast of Corpus Christi was celebrated with a lot of solemnity. During a procession down the streets, the priest, dressed in beautiful vestments, carried the Eucharist in a monstrance. The monstrance was protected by a canopy that some laypeople carried, and some children, dressed as angels, processed on each side of the canopy, throwing flower petals on the ground.

"My mother had a great devotion to the Sacred Heart, and she was in charge of the group of children who threw the flower petals during the procession. She always reserved a place for Lucia. When Aunt

Olimpia took Jacinta to the procession, Jacinta was fascinated to see her cousin, all dressed in white, carrying out such an important function.

"For the next few days, she often went off by herself, picked some flowers, and mimicked the scene, which she so thoroughly enjoyed during the procession. The following year Lucia urged my mother to choose Jacinta also, and she was pleased when my mother did choose her."

"What was Jacinta's reaction?"

"Obviously she was very happy. She anxiously waited for the day. An angel's costume was made for her, and she was told how to toss the flowers.

"Finally, the long-awaited day arrived. The children, dressed as angels, formed a little group and walked in front of the canopy with baskets full of rose petals. Lucia tossed the flowers, but Jacinta wouldn't. Through some signs, my mother tried to make her understand that she should do what the other children were doing, but to no avail. She didn't throw a single petal.

" 'Jacinta, why didn't you throw any flowers to Jesus?' she asked her when the procession was over.

" 'Because I didn't see him,' she replied to Lucia. 'Did you ever see him?'

" 'No. But don't you know that you can't see Jesus in the host? He's the one we receive when we go to Communion.'

" 'And when you go to Communion, do you speak to him?'

" 'Yes.'

" 'But why can't you see him if you speak to him?'

" 'Because he's hidden.'

" 'Why is he hidden?'

"All in all," Fr. Valinho commented, "Jacinta never stopped asking questions. Yet she was able to get a rather precise idea of the nature of the Eucharist, and from that moment on, when she spoke about Jesus, she always spoke about the 'hidden Jesus.' "

The Abbreviated Rosary

"Before the apparitions were verified, did the three cousins have a habit of praying together?" we asked Fr. Valinho.

"Prayer was part of family life. As the children left for the pastures with the sheep, mothers suggested that they find time during the day to recite the rosary. Many did so, especially the girls, who were more receptive to their mothers' suggestions.

"Out in the fields, Lucia, Francisco, and Jacinta prayed the rosary every day, immediately after they finished the frugal lunch they brought with them from home. They prayed voluntarily, but it was tiring. The rosary was a very long prayer for them, especially in light of their strong desire just to play.

"So they invented a certain strategy. They prayed an 'abbreviated' rosary. This way they were able to finish in a few minutes so that they could run and play. This strategy is proof that the three shepherd children were 'normal' children before the apparitions, who liked to play but who still had strong religious feelings in their souls."

"In the history of apparitions, you often find that they seemed to be reserved for children. Why?" we asked Fr. Valinho.

"Well, to be honest, it's only in the last few centuries that those who have been blessed with apparitions have often been children. I remember reading a book about Marian apparitions throughout the two thousand years of Christianity. It contained information on about a thousand apparitions, and there was a statistic concerning the visionaries.

"Up until the year 1200, they were prevalently adult men. There were only five children. During the last hundred years, on the other hand, the prevalence of children has greatly increased: of 450 visionaries, 192 were children, 186 were women, and only 77 were men. Jesus' words in the Gospel come to mind: 'If you do not become like little children, you will not enter the kingdom of heaven.' "

At this point we realized that we had arrived in Fatima. We recognized different streets and buildings. As we entered the town, we drove in front of the large shrine that has been built on the site of the apparitions.

Fr. Valinho asked us to stop. By now it had become a custom. Every time we went in front of the shrine, Fr. Valinho stopped to pray for a few minutes at one end of the square. We stood next to him in silence. Fr. Valinho looked around, then shook his head incredulously.

"And to think that there was nothing here when I was little. Just rocky ground, trees, and hills."

Then he turned to us.

"Well, let's meet here tomorrow morning around ten o'clock. I'll say Mass for the sisters who have their institute in front of that building."

"We'll accompany you home first."

"No, I'll walk, just as I did when I was a child. I need to walk a little bit. We've been sitting in the car for almost the whole day. I'll see you tomorrow."

He smiled at us and slowly walked away. He looked once again at the shrine and acknowledged a woman who recognized him and greeted him. We stayed for a moment as we watched him go, then we headed back to our hotel.

6

THE FIRST CONTACT

People generally use the word "apparition" when they want to indicate that invisible beings become visible in particular situations.

But the term also has a wider meaning. It includes phenomena, occurrences, and events that normally are invisible, inaudible, and incomprehensible but become visible, audible, and comprehensible through the human senses.

The history of religion is filled with such phenomena. But our discussion is limited to Christian belief, and one only has to read the books of the Bible in order to find numerous examples. Angels appear most frequently in order to transmit God's messages and commands to individuals.

The history of the Church and the lives of the saints are studded with apparitions. An apparition is almost always at the origin of the many shrines found throughout the world. Angels, saints, the Blessed Virgin, and Jesus are among those who have appeared, as well as souls of the faithful departed.

People are greatly interested in some of these apparitions even after many years have passed, probably because they have made a deep impression or because the message and the teaching that were transmitted are still very relevant. For this reason, the shrines that were erected in remembrance of an apparition continue to have a strong appeal for believers and attract millions of pilgrims every year.

The shrine at Fatima, however, even though it is a relatively recent shrine, is at the top of the list in popularity. Every year five million pilgrims visit the shrine, and it boasts the highest number of churches, chapels, icons, and altars that have been erected in the world in remembrance of the events that occurred there.

"When people speak about Fatima," Fr. Valinho told us, "they are always referring to the Blessed Mother's apparitions that began on May 13, 1917. In reality, though, others that are no less important preceded those apparitions. They included apparitions of an angel who wanted, in a certain sense, to 'prepare' the visionaries for their encounter with the Virgin Mary, who, in her infinite tenderness, seemed concerned about frightening the three children with her mysterious presence."

Fr. Valinho spoke to us as we stood in front of the shrine, where we had agreed to meet previously.

"It would be very interesting," he continued, "to do a historical study on the manner in which the Virgin Mary's apparitions occurred. She always acts in an extraordinarily delicate, gentle, and tender way as a sign of her great maternal love and care not to disturb souls."

Fr. Valinho spoke with the serenity that is so characteristic of him at every moment of the day.

"My aunt, Sr. Lucia, has told me more than once that when she saw the Virgin Mary, even for the first time, she was never afraid. Her heart was immediately overwhelmed by an immense joy. It couldn't have been otherwise, since a mother never frightens her children."

The First Teacher

Suddenly the story was interrupted. We were standing next to the seventy-foot tower at the shrine, whose carillon, with sixty-three bells, had broken out in a cheerful concert that drowned out our voices. Fr. Valinho signaled us to follow him to the end of the large square where the sound of the bells was not so loud.

"You were saying that the Virgin Mary's apparitions here in Fatima were preceded by those of an angel."

"Yes. There were two different kinds of apparitions: those of the angel and those of the Virgin Mary. In general little is said about these first apparitions, but this is a mistake, because they were very important.

"According to the traditional teaching of the Church, angels are spiritual beings without bodies that are blessed with intelligence, a free will, and a personality. The Old Testament is filled with stories about angels, and even in Jesus' life, angels were always surrounding him. An angel announced the Incarnation, and angels sang at his birth, announced his birth to the shepherds, protected him on his flight into Egypt, served him in the desert, and comforted him during his agony in Gethsemane.

"In Fatima, an angel prepared the children for their important meeting with the Virgin Mary. But he also gave teachings, suggested prayers, and pointed out some important forms of devotion."

"How many times did the angel appear to the three visionaries?"

"Several times. There was a preliminary series of visions that were a little nebulous, in which the angel did not manifest himself clearly and in which he did not speak. It was a kind of overture or gentle approach. Then there were other visions in which the angel was a 'preparatory teacher' for the three visionaries—their guide for what was to happen.

"The first visions can be traced back to the spring of 1915, two years before the Virgin Mary's apparitions, and perhaps even to 1914. My Aunt Lucia has told me that since she didn't go to school, she couldn't count and was unable to distinguish the days of the week and the months of the year. For this reason she wasn't able to establish the exact date when these phenomena began.

"Anyway, whether they started at the end of 1914 or the beginning of 1915, the fact is that the time of preparation for the encounter with the Virgin Mary lasted for at least two years. This information is important for understanding how meticulously and how prudently heaven wanted to prepare the little visionary for such an extraordinary experience."

A Transparent Figure

"As I already said, when word got out that Lucia would start taking the sheep to pasture, several shepherd children in the area offered to accompany her. However, Lucia decided to go with three of her best friends: Teresa Matias, her sister Maria Rosa, and Maria Justino.

"Because of her strong personality and her vivaciousness, Lucia was the leader of the little group, and her companions willingly went along with every decision she made. Therefore, they used to pray for a short while every day after lunch, as her mother had suggested. One day, when they were on a hill at a place called Cabeço, they were praying after they finished eating when they saw something that looked like a human figure stirring gently in the trees."

"What did Sr. Lucia tell you about what she saw?"

"As she herself said, she saw a kind of cloud, whiter than snow, with a human form, like a statue made of snow, that the rays of sun made somewhat transparent. It hovered in the air above the trees. My aunt told me that her friends were a little scared, but she wasn't at all.

"She experienced a certain feeling inside her that she could not explain. The children continued praying and kept their eyes fixed on that figure for the whole time, which did not move and did not speak. It disappeared when they finished praying."

The Foolishness of Children

"When she returned to her home, Lucia didn't say anything to anyone. Most likely she knew that it was something important. But she felt she should keep it to herself and not feed people's curiosity.

"Her friends, however, told their families about it, and news spread throughout the village. Since everyone knew Lucia, she, too, was much criticized. People began to talk about her and laugh at her behind her back. Within a few days, her mother, Maria Rosa, heard the gossip and immediately asked her daughter for an explanation.

" 'People are saying that you saw something—I don't know what— out in the pasture,' she inquired. 'What did you see?'

" 'I don't know,' the child answered.

" 'How can you not know? Your friends have told some incredible stories.'

" 'It looked like a person wrapped in a sheet,' Lucia admitted. 'But I couldn't see either its hands or its eyes.'

" 'The foolishness of children,' Maria Rosa commented.

"It was an expression that in itself might not mean much. But actually anyone who knew my grandmother also knew that it was almost a threat. My grandmother didn't let anyone joke about anything that might in any way be related to religion. No one dared to talk about visions, angels, or things of that sort around her.

"She sensed, however, that it might have been a vision. So my grandmother was already on her guard. Thus, her little comment could easily have been interpreted as a real threat. She was warning her daughter by saying, 'Be careful not to joke about such things.'

"Lucia knew how intransigent her mother was about religion and how loyal she was to the teaching of the Church. An example had occurred a few months before when a new priest was named for the church in Fatima. Fr. Manuel Marques Ferreira came to take the place of Fr. Pena. As soon as the new priest discovered that the people of Fatima were crazy about dancing, he immediately intervened and said that dances were occasions of sin and forbade them.

"The people protested. 'Why was it all right to dance when Fr. Pena was here, and now it's not?' they asked. Even Lucia's sisters raised the question, but their mother, Maria Rosa, cut them short, saying, 'Such questions make no sense. If the priest says we shouldn't dance, it means just that.'"

Gossiping Friends

"Deep in her heart, Lucia probably didn't share her mother's excessive severity and intransigence. Being a child, she was more apt to be carried away by enthusiasm and was more open to other people and to mysterious things. Perhaps this is the reason why she wasn't close to her mother and why she preferred not to say anything about the mysterious apparition."

"What happened?"

"As time went by, the gossip quieted down. But one day, while Lucia and her three shepherd friends were praying, the phenomenon of the mysterious 'presence' happened again. The same faint figure appeared and hovered above the trees without moving and without saying a word.

"Lucia's friends once again talked about it, and the gossip, snickers, and snide remarks started all over. Lucia still remembers that when her sisters would find her quiet and withdrawn, they would ask her, 'Could you be seeing someone wrapped in a sheet?' Then they would begin to laugh at her, and she would feel hurt and humiliated.

"The vision happened even a third time, and for the third time Lucia's friends told everyone about it. The jokes became even worse, and Maria Rosa, who was very worried, summoned her daughter and asked her angrily, 'Do you want to explain this story that's going around?'

" 'I don't know, Mother. I don't know anything,' Lucia answered firmly.

"Maria Rosa was amazed that the little girl was so determined not to say anything. Maybe she was worried. At that point she realized that even if she got angry, she wouldn't find out anything. Lucia had a very strong personality, and once she made up her mind, she wouldn't change it very easily."

"And then?"

"She forgot about it. Lucia realized that the situation could become dangerous. She sensed deep down that those visions were important in some way, and knew that what had happened wasn't over. She probably had a deep intuition or perhaps an inner locution, so she was convinced that the experience should be protected from people's curiosity.

"But her friends, who were a little too talkative, might ruin everything. The best thing was to leave them and find other friends for tending the sheep. Lucia immediately thought about her cousins.

"She got along well with Francisco and Jacinta. At times she did quarrel with Jacinta over stupid little things. But she could trust them. She was the one who went to Aunt Olimpia and insisted that she let Francisco and Jacinta accompany her to the pastures."

"When did this happen?"

"It happened in 1916. Francisco was eight and Jacinta was six. Aunt Olimpia hesitated because Jacinta was still very little, but she decided to let her go because she knew that she would be with her brother. Lucia was thrilled.

"Thus the three children began their new life together as shepherds. They woke up early, ate, made their lunch, and went with the sheep to the pastures. They went to the foot of a hill in a place called Barreiro, where there was a little lake. In order to avoid her old friends yet not go too far away, Lucia almost always chose to go to the fields near her home that belonged to her parents or her aunts and uncles."

The Angel Spoke

"Life was peaceful for Lucia, who blindly trusted her little cousins. Once again the days were beautiful and happy for Francisco and Jacinta, who had longed for the time when they could once again spend all day with Lucia.

"My aunt often told me what kind of shepherd Jacinta was. She said that she was very attentive and very diligent. She loved the sheep. En route to the pasture, she wanted to carry the little sheep that had just been born so they wouldn't get tired on the way. When she arrived at the pasture, she often held them in her arms, petting them and kissing them.

"At the pasture they had to be careful so that the sheep wouldn't wander off and get lost or graze in fields that had been recently planted. But Lucia, Francisco, and Jacinta wanted to have time to play, and they could easily forget about the sheep if they did so. Therefore they decided to spoil them. They started to give them part of their lunch.

The sheep loved the food, especially if it was salty, and grew accustomed to staying nearby the children. Thus, Lucia, Francisco, and Jacinta could play peacefully, knowing that the sheep wouldn't wander away."

"When did the angel appear once again?"

"It was some time after they had been together. It was a genuine apparition in which the angel clearly manifested himself and also spoke. We should go to Cabeço, where this important encounter took place, so that you might better understand. Come on, let's go."

Fr. Valinho took one last glance at the shrine in front of us, as though he wanted to say goodbye to the Blessed Virgin, and set off down the street.

"Are we walking?" we asked, a little alarmed. We wanted to know if we should prepare ourselves for a long walk.

"No, Cabeço is too far from here. We have to go back to Aljustrel. We'll go by car to my sister's house, then we'll continue on foot. You'll find it to be a pleasant walk through green pastures."

7

THE ANGEL

Cabeço is a hilly area. You have to take a little road to get there. The road is paved and well maintained, and passes through groves of olive trees, oak trees, and pine trees. Every once in a while, parcels of land that have been planted with grapes and wheat peek through the trees.

Groups of pilgrims visit this place, praying the rosary or meditating on Jesus' passion and death as they make the stations of a *Via Crucis* ("Way of the Cross") that was donated in 1955 by Hungarian Catholics living in exile. The stations of this *Via Crucis* begin at Cova da Iria and follow the path that Lucia, Francisco, and Jacinta generally took when they led their sheep to pasture. The path passes through Aljustrel and ends on the top of the hill at Cabeço.

There are some marble statues near the top of the hill by the eleventh station, amidst some rocks and stones and next to the twisted trunk of an old olive tree. They depict the three shepherd children of Fatima. An angel stands in front of them.

There was dead silence at the top of the hill overlooking the whole valley. "Once there was a grotto here," Fr. Valinho told us as he pointed to the statues. "There was a cavity in the rocks that was covered by trees.

"On that day, Lucia, Francisco, and Jacinta took their sheep to a piece of land that belonged to my grandparents. You can see it down there, just below us. It is called Chousa Velhai.

"In the middle of the morning it began to rain, and the children decided to climb up here and take shelter in the grotto, while the sheep grazed under the trees. When they got here, it stopped raining. Since they had already climbed up, they didn't want to walk down. So they stayed here and began to play."

Whiter Than Snow

"At noon, they ate lunch as usual and began to pray. While they were praying, a strong wind blew through the trees, which was accompanied by a strange glow. They looked around and saw a little white cloud over the trees on the hill that resembled a human figure. It was coming towards them."

"Did Lucia recognize it?"

"Surely she remembered that it was the same figure that she had seen months before while she was out with her friends. But it was something new for Francisco and Jacinta, and Lucia hadn't told them what she had seen. As the figure approached them, its features became clearer and clearer until it was nearby and they could distinguish a young man who seemed to be fourteen or fifteen years old. 'He was whiter than snow,' Aunt Lucia said, 'so white that the sun made him look transparent, like he was made of glass.' "

"What happened?"

"The figure spoke to the three children. He said, 'Do not be afraid. I am the Angel of Peace. Pray with me.' Kneeling down on the ground, he bowed his head until he touched the ground with his forehead. Then he prayed these words:

" 'My God, I believe, I adore, I hope, and I love you. I ask your forgiveness for those who do not believe, nor adore, nor hope, nor love you.' He invited the children to repeat this prayer with him and prostrate themselves on the ground. They obeyed.

"At this point, they entered a spiritual state of full assent. They immediately learned the words that the angel taught them and were happy to do what he wanted them to do. The angel also told them, 'Pray like that. The hearts of Jesus and Mary will be attentive to the voice of your supplication.' Then he disappeared.

"This time it wasn't a vague vision like the one Lucia had seen a few months before," Fr. Valinho said as he sat on a rock next to the statues of the children. His words resounded amid the prayerful silence of that blessed place and evoked charming images in our minds.

We listened attentively and looked around in amazement. Nature seemed so peaceful and serene. Some little birds were chirping in the branches of the olive trees. We touched the statues. The marble was cold, but we had the strange impression that we were not alone amid the stones.

"The encounter that took place right here, where we are now standing, was very clear and very real," Fr. Valinho reiterated. "The angel approached the three children, appeared before their eyes in a form that could not be mistaken, and spoke to them. Then he gave them a task to do, as though he already considered them to be participants in a project, in a mission. It was definitely an encounter that was much more developed than the initial phenomenon, which Lucia had witnessed almost a year before.

"At that time, the angel's form was not clear. It was like a 'ghost covered by a sheet.' Perhaps he wanted at that time to introduce Lucia to the idea that a vision was possible, so she would not be afraid of something of that nature.

"Now, however, the vision was very distinct. The angel manifested himself and initiated a dialogue. He gave some advice that helped them understand that they were on a journey that was preparing them for other, more important events."

The Beginning of a New Life

"That vision," Fr. Valinho continued, "made a very deep impression on the children. Sr. Lucia told me that she felt 'full of God.' They stood for a long time in silence without moving, because they couldn't even muster up the energy to talk to each other.

"Moreover, they didn't feel the need to do so. They simply repeated over and over again the prayer that the angel had taught them. This strange state continued during the following days. The children could only think about the angel and his words to them.

"Even if the vision only lasted a few minutes, they still felt a deep attachment to it—so strongly and so intimately that the rest of the world was excluded from their thoughts. The only thing that counted was what they had experienced, and nothing else.

"It was to the point that none of the three ever thought of mentioning it to others or of telling their families what had happened. This time the secret remained a secret. There was no problem in this regard."

"Did they obey the angel's request?"

"Of course. In fact, they felt strongly driven to follow what he said. Thus, the desire to pray prostrate on the ground and repeat the words he had taught them was foremost in their minds—above any other thought. They no longer had a desire to play, to run, and to sing. Once the sheep were settled down, they immediately began to pray. They prostrated themselves so many times on the ground that Francisco began to suffer a terrible backache.

"Naturally, all this lasted for a couple of days. Then the inexplicable spiritual atmosphere in which they felt themselves immersed lost its intensity. The children returned to their normal life, playing games, joking, and singing, without ever forgetting the task that was entrusted to them, which was prayer and adoration.

"From that moment on, the angel's visit had changed their way of living and their way of thinking. Several times during the day they prayed as the angel had taught them and relived that marvelous experience, assimilating each time more and more in their hearts."

He Was There, Next to the Well

"The angel's second apparition occurred a few months later," our invaluable guide continued. "Sr. Lucia doesn't know the date, but it must have been in the summer because she remembers that it was very hot and the apparition took place at the well. As I already explained, during the hot months the children returned home with the sheep around ten in the morning, and then left again at five in the afternoon.

"They spent the heat of the day in the house or under the shade of the trees, just like the peasants who worked in the fields. Here it's very hot in the middle of summer. That day, when they returned from the pastures in the morning, they went to the well, which is in a field behind the house."

"Is it the one we can see from here?" we asked, pointing to a nearby well, about three hundred feet from Lucia's house.

"That's the one. It's just as it was back then. It's covered with marble slabs so that people or animals do not fall into it.

"Back then, people drew water from it using one of the piston-style pumps that you don't see much anymore. There was a big olive tree nearby and some fruit trees—plum trees, I seem to recall. My grand-parents called it Arneiro, which means 'sandy place.'

"Lucia, Francisco, and Jacinta went to play and pray there during *siesta* time, as they did every day. Suddenly they saw the strong light that they had already seen at Cabeço, and to their amazement, the angel appeared before their eyes."

"Did he also speak this time?"

"A conversation actually took place.

" 'What are you doing here?' the angel asked. 'Pray, pray much. The most holy hearts of Jesus and Mary have some plans of mercy in regard to you. Continually offer up prayers and sacrifices to the Lord.'

" 'How should we offer sacrifices?' Lucia asked.

" 'You can make sacrifices of all things. Offer sacrifices to God in reparation for all the sins that offend him and as supplication for the conversion of sinners. In this way, try to draw down peace upon your country. I am your guardian angel, the Angel of Portugal. Above all, accept and bear humbly the sufferings that the Lord will send you.'

"Then he disappeared."

The Mystery of Suffering

"It was a brief vision—at least, that's how Aunt Lucia referred to it. But it could have lasted for quite a while. Such spiritual experiences don't have any time limit: sometimes they last a moment that seems like an eternity.

"The angel manifested himself distinctly as he did the time before, and he also described who he was. He might have been the same heavenly messenger from the first apparition, but he described himself using a different name. 'I am the Angel of Portugal,' he said.

"It was a very beautiful revelation, revealing that there aren't guardian angels only for individual persons. Angels are marvelous guides. But we seldom think about them.

"Returning to the visions," Fr. Valinho continued, "it's worth noting that the angel immediately asked, 'What are you doing here?' The three children were playing, but he called them to prayer, as if play for people involved in such important realities was a waste of time. 'Pray. Pray much.'

"Then he added something new concerning everything that was said in the first apparition: 'Offer up sacrifices.' When Lucia asked what kind of sacrifices they should offer, he gave a precise explanation: 'You can make sacrifices to God of all things.' Everything.

"He introduced the children to the mystery of suffering and to the mystery of the Mystical Body. They were innocent children who did not need to do penance for sins they had not committed. But their suffering and their sacrifices would help sinners and would serve as reparation for the injustices committed against God."

"Did the children understand the significance of his words?" we asked.

"Actually, it proved something extraordinary, which Lucia highlighted in her memoirs and which is very important. All three were little children who had come in contact with important realities that surpassed human understanding. They weren't able to understand the profound significance of what the angel was saying.

"But, as Lucia explains, 'the words of the angel were imprinted on our hearts like a light that helped us understand who God was, how much he loved us, and how much he wanted to be loved; how great too was the value of sacrifice and how pleasing it was to him.' Lucia, Francisco, and Jacinta had received some inner illuminations that helped them understand the meaning of some very important truths,

truths that are the essence of human life and Christian teaching.

"Saints spend their lives reflecting and meditating on these truths in an effort to learn something. And these three children, through a special grace that the angel gave them, 'learned' them in a second, and everything was perfectly clear to them. They probably saw and knew what we all will see and know when we are in heaven."

"What did they do after this second vision?"

"The practical consequences were immediate. From that moment on, Lucia, Francisco, and Jacinta began to offer the Lord everything that could be considered as suffering and mortification. While they were tending the sheep, they spent long hours prostrate on the ground, repeating the angel's prayer."

A Wonderful Prayer

"The third apparition again took place here in Cabeço," Fr. Valinho said as he continued his priceless story. "It must have been in October. Around noon, the three children decided to stop at the grotto, which had become sort of a secret hiding place for their prayer times. They were kneeling and were saying over and over the words that the angel had taught them during the first apparition.

"Suddenly, they realized that an intense light was approaching, and soon they saw the angel in front of them. This time he had a chalice in his left hand with a host over it, from which some drops of blood were falling into the chalice. He left the chalice hanging in the air, knelt down next to the children, and taught them a new prayer:

" 'Most Holy Trinity, Father, Son, and Holy Spirit, I offer you the most precious Body, Blood, Soul, and Divinity of Jesus Christ, present in all the tabernacles of the world, in reparation for the outrages, sacrileges, and indifference by which you are offended. By the infinite merits of his Most Sacred Heart and the Immaculate Heart of Mary, I beg for the conversion of all poor sinners.'

"He had the children repeat this prayer three times. Then he got up, took the chalice and the host that were hanging in the air, gave the host to Lucia, and divided the blood in the chalice between Jacinta and Francisco, saying, 'Take the Body and the Blood of Jesus Christ, horribly offended by ungrateful men. Make amends for their crimes and console your God.' Then he prostrated himself again on the ground, repeated the same prayer three times, and disappeared."

"Can you explain the significance of this apparition to us?" we asked our patient guide.

"The third apparition, which Lucia said was of fundamental importance as always, was rich in details. The angel arrived with the Eucharist: the host and the chalice. He didn't say who he was. Probably he didn't need to since he faded into the background before the reality of the Eucharist.

"The three children saw the drops of blood that were falling from the host into the chalice. This little detail helped them understand the close connection between the consecrated Bread and Wine of the Mass.

"Then the angel taught them a new prayer. This time, he addressed the Holy Trinity at length. He started with a word of adoration for the Father, Son, and Holy Spirit, followed by the offering of the 'most precious Body, Blood, Soul, and Divinity of Jesus Christ'—in other words, his redemptive work, which includes the Incarnation, his earthly existence, and his passion and death on the cross."

"He stated that Jesus himself carried out these works. He made it clear that Jesus is present in this way—Body, Blood, Soul, and Divinity—in every tabernacle around the world. The angel taught the children to offer the immense spiritual treasure of this mystery to the Trinity in reparation for the sins that are continually committed by men and women, and to pray for their conversion through the infinite merits of Jesus and of his mother.

"Then the angel 'gave Communion' to the three children. In this third apparition, a ritual was celebrated. The passage from prayer to action or identification took place: the angel and the children acted together and were permeated by prayer and by Christ's presence in the mystery of the Eucharist. It was an extraordinary and amazing vision."

Fr. Valinho seemed inspired as he spoke. He looked at the clear sky. He paused for a long time, perhaps thinking about the importance of those distant events, which happened right where we were standing. We could hear the breeze as it rustled the leaves and broke the silence that surrounded us. We looked up to the top of the hill, where we could see the little village of Aljustrel, Lucia's home.

Many years have passed since those events occurred, but thanks to the story of Fr. Valinho—Sr. Lucia's nephew—a story that he has heard many times directly from the visionary, we have been able to relive those events with an emotion that cannot be described.

And the Children Understood

"As you can see," Fr. Valinho continued, "the angel's three apparitions can be considered a sort of preparation. It's important to understand this so that you do not think that the story surrounding these events is just a nice little children's story. The angel was a teacher, a messenger, who tried to teach the children some higher truths that they, the children, would have to teach the entire world.

"In the first apparition, the angel taught them a prayer. In the second, he taught them the importance of sacrifice. In the third, he presented the mystery of redemption, an event that has shaped the history of the universe."

"Why does God always ask for sacrifices, penance, blood, and suffering, and why does he ask them of innocent children?" we inquired.

"That's a good question," Fr. Valinho answered, as he stopped to think for a moment. "You have to understand why God wanted to redeem man through death on a cross. He could have come into this world bright as the sun, a splendid, victorious warrior. Instead he chose to be a humble carpenter, who ultimately would be condemned like a slave and a criminal.

"This, as I've said, is the mystery of suffering. We'll understand it fully when we are in heaven. But Lucia, Francisco, and Jacinta were blessed with the grace to perceive and understand this mystery when the angel spoke to them about it.

"It is for this reason that they were able to find the strength they needed to be faithful to the teachings that they had received and to persevere in suffering with constancy and a generosity that never ceases to amaze us. They knew and they understood the value of their prayers and their sacrifices. They acted, therefore, out of intense love."

A Strange Exhaustion

"How do you explain the exhaustion the children experienced after each vision of the angel?"

"It's something that is very strange, especially since, as we'll see, this phenomenon didn't occur after Mary's apparitions. The encounter with the angel took every ounce of energy out of the children. But the encounter with the Virgin Mary left them happy, full of strength and joy.

"Some people explain it by saying that, during the encounter with the angel, their human nature came in contact with a totally different nature. Therefore, the children's physical senses and their nervous and emotional systems were affected by an exclusively spiritual entity. This phenomenon was not observed in the encounters with the Virgin Mary.

"This is probably due to the fact that the Virgin Mary is a human creature—a person like us, with a body like ours. Her body is now glorified because Mary is in heaven in body and in soul. So contact during the apparitions was between beings of the same nature, on the same wavelength.

"But there's one other detail that I'd like to mention."

"What is that?"

"I should have pointed it out first, but I'll do so now. Lucia was the only one who spoke with the angel. Jacinta saw him and heard him, while Francisco saw him but didn't hear what the angel said. This also occurred during the apparitions of the Virgin Mary.

"Why? We don't know. Perhaps Francisco wasn't ready for the whole experience, but this is only a conjecture. The fact remains that, even during the angel's apparitions, he did not hear his words. But he still felt totally exhausted just as Lucia and Jacinta did. He was so exhausted that it was only after the second apparition that he told Lucia that he hadn't heard his words.

" 'You spoke with the angel,' he said. 'What did he say?'

" 'You didn't hear?' his cousin asked.

" 'No. I saw you speaking to him. I heard what you said to him. But I don't know what he said to you.'

"Francisco asked Lucia this question a few hours after the second apparition, which took place at the well. But the supernatural atmosphere in which the angel had left the three children had not completely disappeared, and Lucia told Francisco that she would explain it to him the following day. The famous exhaustion that she experienced prevented her from talking.

"The next day, as soon as he saw her, Francisco asked, 'Did you sleep last night? I could only think about the angel.' Then Lucia told him what the angel had said during the first and second apparitions.

"Francisco didn't seem to understand very well and asked her a lot of questions. 'Who is the Almighty? What does it mean to say that the hearts of Jesus and Mary are attentive to our supplications?'

"Lucia tried to explain, but Francisco was still full of doubts."

8

The Beautiful Lady

May 13, 1917, was a Sunday. Francisco, Jacinta, and Lucia woke up early and went to the parish church for the first Mass of the day, which was celebrated at daybreak. They returned home, ate breakfast, and left with the sheep, just as they did every day.

It had been several months since the last apparition of the angel. Even though the visits had occurred on three different occasions in 1916, from all visible appearances nothing had changed in the lives of the three children. They had succeeded in keeping the apparitions secret and had not even spoken about them with their family. Yet their souls were deeply marked by them.

Because of the absence of any external signs that indicated otherwise, most biographers have mistakenly written that Lucia, Francisco, and Jacinta resumed their normal life of games and play within a few months after the angel's last apparition, and had completely forgotten what had happened. According to Fr. José Valinho, this is not true.

They Did Not Forget

We picked up Fr. Valinho at his sister's house, where he had spent the night. He wanted to take us to the places where the Blessed Mother had appeared. Before leaving the hotel, we had read a few chapters of a book that recounted the story of Fatima. We stopped right at the point where it said the three visionaries had forgotten about the angel's apparitions—in May of 1917. We told Fr. Valinho about what we had read, and he responded rather decisively.

"No, they did not forget. There is no way in which the three children could have forgotten about what happened, especially given the fact that the angel urged Lucia, Francisco, and Jacinta to pray every day the prayer that he taught them. And they did. Thus, there was continuity in their deeds, an ongoing link.

"Every time they prayed those prayers, they remembered the visions, heard once again the voice of the heavenly messenger, saw once again his luminous figure, and experienced once again the same joy and enthusiasm as they had before. It was as if the whole mysterious experience, including its gift of grace, was repeating itself. This happened daily. It could happen several times a day.

"Moreover," Fr. Valinho emphasized, "from the end of 1916 to May of 1917, several changes occurred in my grandmother's house that encouraged the three visionaries, especially Lucia, to reflect and pray. The angel had urged them to 'accept and endure without complaining the suffering that the Lord sends you.' Within a short time, they felt the suffering."

"Where Has the Joy Gone?"

"During the year 1916," Fr. Valinho continued, "Lucia's two older sisters got married and left their parents' home in order to start their own families. My mother, who was the oldest, was the first to get married and move out. Then it was Maria Teresa's turn. They didn't live very far away, but they were no longer at home with their mother."

"But was there any real suffering per se?" we asked.

"At that time something unfortunate happened to my grandfather. Lucia reflected upon it in her memoirs. She wrote that her 'father let himself be dragged into some bad company and fell into the trap of a sad passion, as a result of which we had already lost some of our lands.'

"Lucia's words are, perhaps, somewhat exaggerated. By 'sad passion,' she meant that her father drank a little. It was partially true, but nothing too dramatic. My grandfather did have some problems. He didn't get along very well with the new pastor of the parish, and he no longer went to Mass at the parish. Instead he went to the Mass every Sunday in Vila Nova de Ourem."

"What happened?"

"This affected the family. At that time, my grandfather began to neglect his work in the fields. As a result, there were some economic problems. In the face of such an emergency, my grandmother had to send her two other daughters, Gloria and Carolina, to work as maids. At that time a maid stayed at her employer's house day and night, so it felt as though the two girls moved out."

"Were these changes in the family noticeable?"

"Very noticeable. Maria dos Anjos and Teresa were married. Maria Gloria and Maria Carolina were working. With the presence of five young girls who were full of life, the house had always seemed to resound with cheerful song, laughter, and jokes. Now the house seemed like a tomb.

"My grandmother was so sad that she felt as if she were going to die. Often, as she waited for her husband and for her son, Manuel, to return from the fields in the evening, she was overwhelmed with sadness. Looking at the table set for dinner and seeing her daughters' four empty places, she began to cry and ask, 'My God, where has the joy gone from this house?' Furthermore, Manuel expected to be drafted at any moment into the army, and with a war looming on the horizon, my grandmother's worries were even greater."

"What was Lucia's reaction?"

"Lucia, even though she was a child, sensed how serious the situation was. She suffered because of her family's situation but confronted the problems by putting into practice what the angel had suggested. She offered her suffering for the conversion of sinners. When her discouragement was too overwhelming, she would go to the well so that her mother wouldn't see her and become even more upset. There, she knelt on the ground and cried and cried."

Intense Preparation

"This clearly demonstrates that the angel's teachings were deeply rooted in Lucia's heart," we commented. "She hadn't forgotten them. They were bearing fruit."

"Exactly," Fr. Valinho agreed. "Guided by grace, Lucia was walking on the road to perfection. The same thing was happening to Francisco and Jacinta.

"Lucia said that her two cousins were suffering along with her. They were at her side, trying to comfort her and sharing her burdens. They used to see her at the well.

"Because of her sorrow and tears, she was unable to talk and explain to them what was happening. But her two cousins understood, and they also wept. At that time, Lucia recalls, Jacinta prayed their offering aloud, 'My God, as an act of reparation for the conversion of sinners, we offer you all these sufferings and sacrifices.' "

"How long did this situation last?"

"The dos Santos family's sufferings continued for a long time, and even got worse. My grandmother got sick, and Aunt Gloria and Aunt Carolina had to return home to take care of her and the house. The doctors prescribed different medicines for my grandmother, but they didn't help her.

"The pastor of the parish was moved to pity and wanted to take her to Leiria in his own mule-driven cart so some other doctors could examine her. My grandmother went to Leiria, accompanied by my Aunt Teresa. It was an exhausting trip, and she returned home half-dead. The doctors examined her and discovered that she had a lesion on her heart, a ruptured disc on her spine, and kidney problems. They prescribed some painful remedies.

"So you can see," Fr. Valinho commented, "how the months following the angel's apparition and preceding those of the Virgin Mary were months of trial and suffering for Lucia and also for Francisco and Jacinta. All three consciously experienced this. Based on the teachings they received from the angel, they offered their suffering to God. Thus, it was a time of intense prayer and great love for the Lord.

"Prayer is a dialogue between the creature and the Creator, a 'living' dialogue that always produces concrete results in a person's spirit. To understand the value of prayer, you have to be fully aware that it is essentially an action between two persons: the person who is praying and the person who is listening. Lucia, Francisco, and Jacinta were overwhelmed by painful situations but prayed intensely and offered their suffering to God for sinners. They were performing, therefore, a great act of love.

"God, who is truly a Father, saw their sacrifices and listened to their prayers with great love. He responded with graces and spiritual gifts. The Virgin Mary, Jesus, and the angels cared for the three children with infinite affection.

"During those months, a spiritual ferment was taking place here in

Aljustrel between heaven and earth, which fostered an understanding of heavenly things and supernatural values in the three children. It was intense preparation for the events that would eventually occur. When May 13, 1917, arrived, Lucia, Francisco, and Jacinta were well prepared for their important encounter."

"Everything Began Here"

As we have already pointed out, May 13 occurred on a Sunday. Lucia met Francisco and Jacinta and decided that they would take the sheep to graze at Cova da Iria, located on some property that belonged to their parents.

Nature produced an explosion of colors and fragrances. Blessed by the sun and the spring rain, they burst out everywhere. The fields, the meadows, and even the woods in the hills were filled with flowers and fresh herbs. It was a pleasure to take the sheep to pasture because there was plenty of tasty food on which they could graze.

"Today Cova da Iria is in the center of Fatima. But at that time it was an open field, surrounded by some little woods. It was a perfect pasture. The children only had to be careful that the sheep did not graze where crops had been planted.

"It's good that we're going to Cova da Iria so that you might better understand what happened there that day," Fr. Valinho told us. We drove to the heart of Fatima, where the large shrine is located, as well as the little chapel in front where the apparitions took place.

We left our car in a parking lot near the shrine and walked to the square. It was ten o'clock in the morning, but there were already many pilgrims there. There were probably ten to fifteen thousand people in the square, but it did not seem like there were that many. They got lost in the sunny expanse.

"You have to remember that when I was a child, there were only open fields," Fr. Valinho said. "A chapel was constructed on the site of the apparitions with the offerings that the first pilgrims made, but it was blown up on March 6, 1922, by an anticlerical group. Afterwards, another chapel was built on the ruins of the first, which has now been incorporated into the cement and glass structure that Pope John Paul II dedicated on May 13, 1982. Follow me. Let's get closer."

The little chapel is located on the left when you are looking at the shrine. It is an overwhelming experience to know that you are standing on the spot where the apparitions took place. We looked around for the hill where the Virgin stood, but we did not see any trace of it. Devout pilgrims have entirely removed it, taking little bits of the soil home with them as relics.

The chapel was filled with people who were there for Mass. We stood at a distance in order not to disturb them.

"Everything began here," Fr. Valinho whispered. "Lucia, Francisco, and Jacinta arrived here around noon. They walked slowly so that the sheep could graze on the fresh grass on the way. Then they chose a quiet spot where they could eat the lunch they had brought with them.

"After they finished eating, they prayed the rosary, as they did every day. But they no longer prayed it as they used to, saying only the first words of the Hail Mary. They recited the prayers in their entirety and with great devotion, as the angel had encouraged them to do.

"When they finished praying, they began to play. They were thinking about building a little wall out of some stones next to a bush that would be a little house. While they were working, there was a flash of lightning.

" 'We'd better go home. Maybe a storm is coming,' Lucia said.

" 'Yes, let's go,' the other two answered."

"Brighter Than the Sun"

"They began to gather the sheep and walk down the hill. Everything here is flat now, but I remember very well how the countryside used to be. There was a depression in the ground here that was later filled with thousands of cubic feet of earth. So the three children walked down and led the sheep along the path to their home.

"When they arrived in this area, more or less there where the priest is now celebrating Mass, there was another big flash of lightning. They looked around, expecting it to rain any minute. There, where there is now a statue of the Blessed Virgin, they saw a lady standing over a little oak tree.

"Lucia gave a magnificent description of her that reveals all the wonder she experienced standing before such a beautiful woman: 'She was a lady who was clothed in white, brighter than the sun, and she radiated a light that was brighter and stronger than that of a crystal vase filled with clear water, through which the brilliant rays of sun are shining.'

"The three children," Fr. Valinho continued, "were right next to the lady. You see, often when people tell the story of the apparitions, they say that the Virgin Mary appeared on a little holm oak, without saying anything else. So people who hear the story think that the Virgin Mary stood on a beautiful tree full of leaves, at least thirty or forty feet away from the visionaries.

"She certainly could have done so, because this area was full of big trees. Instead, she chose a little tree that was only about three feet tall according to those who saw it. She was very close to the faces of the three children. She was right in front of them.

"Lucia, in her memoirs, specified that the distance separating her and the Blessed Virgin was only about five feet. I personally think it is important to emphasize this point. It helps us understand how the Virgin Mary presented herself humbly, in all simplicity, showing the children affection, tenderness, and trust. This is why they were not in the least bit afraid and why they felt caught up in the light that emanated from the apparition."

"What happened at that point?"

"The Lady said, 'Do not be afraid. I will not harm you.'

" 'Where do you come from?' Lucia asked.

" 'I come from heaven.'

" 'What do you want of me?'

" 'I have come to ask you to come here for six consecutive months, at this same hour, on the thirteenth day of each month. Then I will tell you who I am and what I want. Then I will return a seventh time.'

" 'Will I also go to heaven?' Lucia asked.

" 'Yes, you will go there.'

" 'And Jacinta?'

" 'She, too.'

" 'And Francisco?'

" 'He, too, but he will have to pray many rosaries.'

"My aunt has said that the conversation was very elementary. It was very basic, but extremely important. First of all, it shows that the children, even when confronted with such an extraordinary event, did not experience any fear or any feeling of apprehension, anxiety, uncertainty, or insecurity."

"How was that possible?" we asked, a little perplexed.

"If you think about it, it's only natural. How could a mother frighten her children? Lucia has emphasized this several times. After the flash of lightning, they were afraid at first that they would be caught in a storm out in the fields with the sheep. But as soon as they saw the lady, all their fears disappeared."

"Yes, We Will"

"Upon hearing that the lady came from heaven," Fr. Valinho continued, "Lucia asked right away if she and her cousins would go there. Back then, especially among the people in the rural areas, knowing where you were going to end up was an issue that was often discussed. Priests often preached about heaven, hell, and purgatory, and the children understood very well this whole issue. They were afraid of hell and curious about heaven.

"Lucia, when she found herself face-to-face with the lady from heaven, asked right away if she and her cousins would one day go to heaven. But she didn't stop there. Once she had the answer, she insisted on knowing more.

"A short time before, two girls from Aljustrel, whom she had known well, had died. One of the girls used to spend time with her family learning how to weave. Immediately Lucia asked frankly and confidently for information on her friend.

" 'Is Maria das Neves already in heaven?'

" 'Yes, she's there.'

" 'And Amelia?'

" 'She's in purgatory.'

"This was another brief dialogue that was rich in content. One of the two girls was already in heaven. The other was in purgatory. The reality of purgatory was confirmed with a very short sentence.

"Then the lady asked, 'Will you offer sacrifices to God and accept all the sufferings that he will send you in reparation for the sins that have offended him and as supplication for the conversion of sinners?'

"The lady," Fr. Valinho commented, "confronted them with the essence of the mission that she wanted to give these innocent little children. They responded with the generosity that had already distinguished them from others.

" 'Yes, we will.'

" 'You will, therefore, have to suffer much, but the grace of God will be your comfort.' "

Drunk With Happiness

"At this point, something extraordinary and very important happened. Lucia recalls that 'upon saying these words, the Virgin Mary opened her hands, which gave off a very intense light, a sort of reflection that came from her, and penetrated us to the depths of our souls, causing us to see ourselves in God, who was that light, more clearly than we see ourselves in a radiant mirror. Then, through an intimate impulse that had been communicated to us, we fell to our knees and earnestly repeated, "Most Blessed Trinity, I adore you. My God, My God, I love you in the Most Blessed Sacrament." ' "

"The same thing happened during the angel's apparition," we commented.

"Exactly. At that time, too, through an intense light, the three children were able to understand supreme spiritual truths. Now the light that enveloped them helped them see their God and the truth of their being in God. These are very deep, spiritual intuitions that left them quite disturbed. As the angel had taught them, they prostrated themselves and prayed."

"How did the apparition end?"

"After a while, the lady added, 'Pray the rosary every day to obtain peace in the world and an end to the war.' Then she began to rise up serenely, going up in the sky until she disappeared.

"The three children were silent. They experienced an intense joy in their hearts but didn't speak. Contrary to what had happened to them when the angel had appeared to them, they did not feel exhausted and drained of all their energy. In fact, they experienced much happiness and a strong desire to move about—to run and play—in order to express outwardly the fire they felt within.

" 'What a beautiful lady,' Jacinta said aloud, her face radiant.

" 'Do you want to bet,' Lucia said suspiciously, 'that you'll tell everyone what happened?'

" 'No, I won't say anything. Don't worry,' she replied in a soft voice."

9

Suspicion and Mistrust

At sunset on May 13, 1917, Lucia, Francisco, and Jacinta gathered the sheep and began to walk home. They walked next to the sheep, silently engrossed in their thoughts. They were trying to absorb everything that had happened.

Every now and then Jacinta said to herself, "What a beautiful woman!"

"I suggest that you don't say anything to anyone," Lucia immediately injected.

"No, no. You can be sure I won't tell anyone," Jacinta answered.

Lucia was ten years old. She was a good and simple child. But she did not trust adults. For this reason, she asked her cousins to keep it a secret.

She remembered quite well what had happened after the angel's apparitions two years before, when she had been out in the pasture with her three friends, Teresa Matias, Maria Rosa Matias, and Maria Justino. The girls had spoken about it, and the whole village had laughed at them. Her sisters had teased her for months.

"She'll Tell Everyone"

"What a beautiful woman," Jacinta repeated as she clapped her hands for joy.

"Did you hear her?" Francisco asked. He probably understood Lucia's concern since he was older. "Wait and see; she'll tell everyone as soon as we get home."

"I certainly will not," Jacinta protested.

"We'll see," Lucia said under her breath.

She was worried. This time she also sensed that not everything would go smoothly. Jacinta was too little to understand how important it was to be discreet about something so outside the ordinary.

She had conducted herself well after the angel's apparition and had not spoken to anyone. But now Jacinta appeared too excited and too joyful. She seemed as if she were going to explode because she was so happy. Lucia felt as if the little girl would say something.

"I advise you not to say anything to anyone," Lucia repeated for the umpteenth time when they arrived in Aljustrel and when Francisco and Jacinta were walking toward the sheep pen.

"Not even to Aunt Olimpia," she added, looking her cousin straight in the eyes.

"I promised you I won't say anything," the little girl answered. She was undaunted by her cousin's penetrating look.

Lucia continued on her way. She arrived at her own home and put the sheep in their pen. She went inside and kissed her mother with the same passion and affection as always.

Maria Rosa was busy making dinner. She realized, though, that her daughter was unusually silent.

"Do you feel all right?" she asked.

"I'm fine, perfectly fine, Mama," Lucia answered, smiling.

Manuel and her father arrived. They ate dinner together, chatting as usual. Lucia helped her mother clear the table and wash the dishes. Then she went out in front of the house.

It was already dark. The soft spring air felt good on her skin. She could see the first stars in the sky.

Lucia stood looking up at the sky, as she often did with her cousins when they played "count the angels' lamps." This evening, however, she was thinking about other things. She could still see in her mind the image of that beautiful lady who had disappeared in the infinite distance of the sky.

"I Saw the Blessed Virgin"

"Lucia, wake up. It's time." Her mother's voice woke her up from her pleasant and refreshing sleep. As always, she jumped out of bed and began to get dressed quickly. She had breakfast, fetched the sheep, and headed to Barreiro. Francisco and Jacinta had already arrived. Francisco ran up to her with a worried look on his face.

"Jacinta told everything," he said with a sad look as he nodded at his little sister.

"I knew it," Lucia answered.

"Something inside me wouldn't let me keep quiet," Jacinta pleaded and began to cry.

"It's all right," Lucia said gently. "Don't cry now. But don't tell anyone anything else. Above all, you shouldn't tell anyone what the lady told us."

"But I already have."

"What did you say?"

"That the lady promised to take us to heaven right away."

"That's what you told them!"

"I'm sorry; I won't say anything else to anybody."

By now the damage had been done. Lucia had advised them to be quiet the day before because she sensed that they were experiencing something very special yet very delicate that people would not be able to understand. She knew that when they learned about it, they would laugh. This would displease her mother, who was very strict when it came to such matters. At this point, though, it was too late.

"Jacinta spoke about it because of the tremendous joy that she had in her heart," Fr. Valinho explained. Moreover, since she was accustomed to trusting her mother completely and telling her everything, she simply could not understand why she should be quiet about something so important and so beautiful.

"So when she arrived at the house and Francisco was still outside, Jacinta ran to the kitchen looking for her mother. However, she had not yet arrived back from the market in Batalha, where she had gone with her husband. Jacinta sat at the door and waited. As soon as she saw her parents, she ran to meet them.

"She threw herself in her mother's arms, saying, 'Mama! Today I saw the Blessed Virgin.'

" 'How lucky,' Aunt Olimpia answered with a smile. 'So the Blessed Mother came to you. You must be a little saint!'

"Jacinta was mortified and followed her mother into the house repeating, 'But I saw her. I really saw her,' and began to tell her in detail what had happened at Cova da Iria."

Giving Their Snack to the Sheep

The day after the apparition, the three little shepherds returned with their sheep to Cova da Iria. They felt forced to do so by a secret, irresistible nostalgia. In the depths of their hearts, they thought they might see the mysterious lady again, but it was a tremendous joy even to see the little oak tree where she had stood.

They guided the sheep to the back of the slope and stood silently at the place of the apparition. Jacinta stood back at a distance. Lucia thought she might still feel guilty for having betrayed their secret pact.

"Jacinta, come and play," she said.

"I don't want to play today," the little girl replied.

"Why not?"

"The lady told us to say the rosary and to offer sacrifices for the conversion of sinners. We should pray."

"And offer sacrifices," Francisco added.

"How do we offer them?" Jacinta asked.

"We can give our snack to the sheep," Francisco suggested.

They all felt it was a good idea.

"From that day on," Fr. Valinho explained, "the three children began to put into practice what the lady said. Often they fasted. They gave their snack to the sheep and satisfied their hunger with food that did not taste very good.

"They ate acorns, pine nuts, bellflower roots, mulberries, mushrooms, wild fruit, and olives. Even when choosing such unappetizing food, they tried to practice mortification. Instead of eating nuts from trees that were sweet-tasting, they chose ones that were bitter-tasting."

"Did this penance of giving their snack to the sheep last for very long?"

"One day they met some children from a neighboring village on the road who were begging. Jacinta suggested that they give their snack to these children instead of giving it to the sheep. They continued to do so every day. The poor children became accustomed to receiving help from them and started to wait for them. As soon as they saw the little shepherds, they ran to meet them."

"Do you think Jacinta was the most determined?"

"My aunt, Sr. Lucia, says that little Jacinta seemed insatiable when it came to making sacrifices for the conversion of sinners. She not only deprived herself of meals, but she also went thirsty. On certain days, the weather was extremely hot and dry, especially in the mid-afternoon. At such times, thirst becomes a real torture. The three children resisted.

"One day they felt as if they were going to faint, so Lucia decided to go to the house of a nearby family and ask for some water. They also gave her some bread. When she returned to her friends, she was happy.

"She gave Francisco the jug so he could drink, and he answered, 'I don't want a drink.'

" 'Why not?' Lucia asked.

" 'I want to suffer for the conversion of sinners,' Francisco said.

" 'Here, you drink, Jacinta,' Lucia said, offering the pitcher to the little girl.

" 'I too want to suffer for the conversion of sinners,' Jacinta replied.

"Lucia didn't want to do any less than her cousins. She, too, decided not to take a drink. She poured the water into a natural basin of a rock and called the sheep. They quickly drank it up because they, too, were very thirsty. Then she returned the jug.

"The heat that day grew stronger and stronger. The din of the crickets and the frogs was so loud that it was almost deafening. Jacinta, who normally loved to listen to their concert, felt so dazed from fatigue that she said to Lucia, 'Please tell the grasshoppers and frogs to be quiet. They're giving me such a headache.' "

A Great Sorrow

Meanwhile, the story of the apparition was spreading among the people of Aljustrel and Fatima. Olimpia, who was Jacinta and Francisco's mother, was not too concerned after she heard her daughter's account. Yet she knew that her daughter never told lies. Therefore, she thought that something extraordinary must have happened at Cova da Iria.

Olimpia went to see Mrs. dos Santos, Lucia's mother. "My daughter didn't say anything to me," Maria Rosa answered, amazed and surprised. Olimpia also spoke with her neighbors, merely out of curiosity, and did not attach any importance to the incident.

The story was so sensational that news spread throughout the whole area within a short time. People were talking about it. Some laughed while others criticized. Some attributed it to the excessive devotion with which Maria Rosa had brought up her children.

Maria Rosa was annoyed. The whole story touched upon a very serious matter. Hearing all the superficial small talk among the people, she realized that the matter was more serious than she had initially thought. She was sure that it was something the children had dreamed up.

"It's impossible that the Virgin Mary would appear to one of my children," she said to herself. "Lucia and the other two are making up stories."

Maria Rosa summoned Lucia. "What is this that I'm hearing?" she asked.

"What are you hearing?"

"Jacinta said that you saw the Virgin Mary."

Lucia bowed her head and did not answer.

"Put an End to the Whole Story"

"My grandmother was very strict with her children," Fr. Valinho related. "My mother said that my grandmother was ready to turn a blind eye to nearly everything, but not to dishonesty. Lying for her was the worst thing. Therefore, she was thrown into deep confusion because of Lucia's reaction, which affirmed the vision.

"Since my grandmother was a very religious woman, she suffered terribly over the idea that Lucia was deceiving people on matters pertaining to religion. 'Such a terrible thing had to happen to me,' she said repeatedly. 'I already have enough problems with my health, and now there's this disgrace. Having a daughter who lies is the worst problem.'

"But she wasn't satisfied with just complaining. As the days went by, the people of Fatima were talking about the event and were pointing at the visionaries' parents. Rumors had also spread to neighboring villages. My grandmother felt as if she were going to die from embarrassment. She decided to put an end to the whole story."

"How?"

"She wanted Lucia to admit that she made up the whole thing. Every day she pestered her daughter, telling her that she should retract everything she said and that she should go around to the villages asking people for forgiveness and telling them that she had invented everything.

" 'I can't because I really did see that lady,' Lucia said. But my grandmother insisted, raising her voice—something that she did only when she was exasperated.

" 'I can't or I would be lying,' Lucia repeated, thinking that this would make her mother stop and think. But it was worthless. Anger got the best of my grandmother, and she grabbed a broom and beat her daughter with it. She didn't worry about whether she was hurting her.

"Lucia cried in despair but would not give in because she didn't want to be a liar. When Francisco and Jacinta visited their cousin and saw that she was crying and that she was sore from the blows she had received, they cried along with her. Jacinta did so more than her brother. She said over and over, 'I'm the cause of all this.'

" 'Yes, you are,' Francisco scolded her, making her feel even worse. However, Lucia tried to console her."

"How did Francisco and Jacinta's parents react?"

"They were more understanding," Fr. Valinho explained. "Especially Uncle Marto. He was a simple and wise man. One day he said, 'These children cannot be lying. They've never done so, and there's no reason for them to lie about something so sensitive.'

"He believed them from the beginning. But he never showed any enthusiasm that might appear out of place. His wife, on the other hand, was detached from the whole thing, and never turned against her daughter as my grandmother, Maria Rosa, did."

"And Lucia's sisters?"

"They were young and carefree, and they didn't believe them either. My mother, for example, thought the whole thing was impossible and never could understand how Lucia could make up such a tale. For this reason, she just watched how things unfolded and tried to understand her sister's behavior. As June 13 drew closer, gossip increased. Everyone was curious to see what would happen."

10

THE GREAT PROMISE

Maria Rosa repeatedly told her children, "Let's trust in St. Anthony."

St. Anthony was the patron saint of the parish church in Fatima and the patron saint of Portugal. His feast day was one of the most important days in the country. The Church celebrated this important religious event with solemnity and splendor. There was a High Mass in the morning, and a well-known preacher would come from the city to preach on the life of St. Anthony.

In the afternoon his statue was carried in procession around the town. The celebration continued with music, dancing, and singing. Ox-driven carts were decorated with flowers and green branches, and treats were distributed to the people. In the evening, there were fireworks and shooting. All the young men and women dressed up in their most beautiful clothing and spent the entire afternoon in the town square.

Maria Rosa knew that these glittering festivities fascinated Lucia. Therefore, she hoped that the feast of St. Anthony would divert her attention from that ridiculous meeting she said she had had with the mysterious lady at Cova da Iria.

"Come With Us to See the Blessed Mother"

The Martos shared her hope. Olimpia and her husband, Manuel, even if they seemed not to be very concerned by the whole matter, watched the behavior of their two children, Francisco and Jacinta, with fear and concern.

"What should we do?" Olimpia asked her husband as June 13 approached.

"What *should* we do?" Manuel Marto answered with uncertainty. It did not seem right to go to Cova da Iria with their children. Their presence might lend importance to something that might simply be a figment of the children's imagination. But their absence might be interpreted as indifference, and Jacinta, who was so attached to her parents, would probably feel bad.

The little girl felt that her mother's presence at the upcoming meeting was important. "Mother, you have to come with us to see the Blessed Mother," she continually repeated with confidence and enthusiasm.

"What Blessed Mother? You silly little thing," Olimpia answered. "We have to celebrate the feast of St. Anthony!"

"I'm going to Cova da Iria."

"There's music, treats, and fireworks at our feast. Don't you remember how much fun we had last year?"

"But the Blessed Mother will be at Cova da Iria."

"But no one will see her."

"The Blessed Mother said she would come. Certainly you will see her."

Jacinta spoke with such certainty and so freely that Olimpia felt she could no longer continue to contradict her. She was getting tired of it.

"What will we do, then?" the Martos repeatedly asked each other.

Finally, Manuel thought of a diplomatic solution. For some time he had needed to buy a couple of oxen. On June 13 there was an important exhibition in Pedreira, an agricultural center not far from Fatima.

"We'll go to the exhibition," he told his wife. "That way there will be a reason for our absence and the children won't be hurt."

The Second Appointment

Maria Rosa dos Santos had given orders to her daughters not to mention Cova da Iria.

"By continuing to talk to Lucia about that whole thing," she told her family, "we're just reminding her about it. If we're quiet, she might even forget about it. Let's speak to her about the feast of St. Anthony instead. She loves celebrations, and maybe she'll get all excited about it as in past years."

In the meantime, Lucia did not express what she was thinking. She seemed happy and peaceful. She had met with some of her friends and had made plans to go with them to Fatima on the morning of the thirteenth. She picked out an elegant dress from her wardrobe that she especially liked, brushed it, and hung it outside to air.

Maria Rosa immediately informed her married daughters. They all uttered a sigh of relief. They were sure that Lucia could not resist the attraction of the saint's feast day.

In reality, Lucia was thinking about her appointment with the lady. On the evening of June 12, when they were returning with the sheep, she told her cousins, "Tomorrow morning we'll take the sheep to Valinhos. There's plenty of fresh grass there. The sheep will have finished grazing within a couple of hours, so we will be able to take them home and then go to Cova da Iria."

They did just that. When Jacinta woke up, she ran to her mother's room to ask her once again to go to Cova da Iria, but she found her bed empty. "Mother and Father left early. They had to go to the exhibition in Pedreira to buy some oxen," one of her sisters told her. Jacinta did not complain. She knew that her parents had to take care of their business.

It was a very hot day. Valinhos was close to the village, and it took only a few minutes to get there. While the sheep were intently grazing, the three little shepherds prayed the rosary. They wanted to talk, but they did not know what to say. They were already growing anxious about reliving the indescribable experience of the month before.

Around nine o'clock, Lucia's brother, Manuel, arrived. "There are some people who want to speak to you," he said. Lucia decided to return home early. She gathered together the sheep. "I'll see you at Cova da Iria," she told her two cousins.

People had arrived from the neighboring villages, where word had spread about the apparitions. They were curious. They wanted to see her and be near to her.

"I have to go to Fatima to see some friends," Lucia told her mother.

"She Needs the Broomstick"

Maria Rosa was overjoyed when she heard these words. Lucia changed in a hurry. She put on the dress that she had prepared, along with some new shoes. She arranged a white scarf on her head. She looked beautiful.

She said goodbye to her mother and headed to Fatima. Her friends were waiting for her at the church—a little group of fourteen girls. They already were aware of everything. They greeted their friend with affection and headed off with her to Cova da Iria. One of Lucia's sisters witnessed the scene and ran to tell her mother.

"It seemed too good to be true," Maria Rosa exclaimed. She took a shawl and ran out. She felt she needed to keep an eye on her daughter, if only from a distance. With all the gossip about the apparition, she had noticed the angry looks some of the people in the area gave her daughter.

When some women saw her go by, they would comment, "She needs the broomstick," or, "If she were my daughter, I would straighten her out." She had heard about these comments, and it was very painful for her.

She was afraid that someone would hurt her Lucia. She was afraid too that they might be mean to her and make her suffer. She knew that Francisco and Jacinta's parents had gone to Pedreira. Therefore, the three children were alone and defenseless.

She had to be near them in order to keep the situation under control. "I'll keep my distance and hide," she told herself. "But I want to be there."

Along the way she met people from other villages who were going to Cova da Iria. She kept her distance, fearing that someone would recognize her. When she arrived, she saw a little crowd of fifty people.

Lucia was in the middle, and Francisco and Jacinta were next to her. They were near a little holm oak, talking to some people around them. Perhaps Lucia was telling them what had happened the month before.

The air was stuffy. Lucia went and sat down a short distance away in the shade of a tall tree. Some people offered her some oranges. She took one but did not eat it.

Then, around noon, she knelt down with Francisco and Jacinta by her side. Those who were present imitated her. Lucia's friends stood nearby, and one of them began to recite the rosary.

At a certain point, Lucia interrupted their prayer, turned to her cousin, and said, "Jacinta, the Blessed Mother is coming. I saw the flash of lightning." The three little shepherds then stood up and ran to the little oak tree, followed by the other people.

Immersed in Light

The lady was already there. A dialogue took place, which Lucia herself revealed.

"You commanded us to come here. Please tell us what you want," Lucia said.

"I want you to come here on the thirteenth of next month, to recite the rosary every day, and to learn how to read. Then I will tell you what else I want."

Lucia remembered a sick person who had asked for prayers, and the Blessed Virgin answered, "If he is converted, he will be healed within the year."

"I want to ask you to take us to heaven," Lucia said.

"Yes," the lady answered. "I will soon come to take Jacinta and Francisco. But you must remain here longer. Jesus will use you to make me better known and more loved. He wishes to establish throughout the world devotion to my Immaculate Heart."

"Then I shall remain alone?"

"No, my child. You are suffering very much, but do not get discouraged. I will never forsake you. My Immaculate Heart will be your refuge and the way that will lead you to God."

When she said these words, the lady parted her hands, and for the second time the three children were immersed in an intense light. In front of the palm of Mary's right hand was a heart crowned with thorns that seemed to pierce it.

Lucia got up in a hurry, pointed to the sky, and said to those present, "See, there she goes." After a few seconds she added, "Now you cannot see her anymore. She has entered heaven, and the doors are already closed."

People walked up to the little oak tree and pointed to the little branches. Whereas they had been straight before, they now were bent, just as they would be under weight.

Obviously the people were deeply moved. They began to pull off little branches and leaves. "Take the leaves from the branches that are underneath," Lucia said. "Don't touch those where Our Lady stood."

"There Is No Comparison"

This is an account of the facts as recorded, thanks to the many times that the events have been reconstructed since then. But we wanted to understand better the meaning of this apparition. So we asked Fr. Valinho.

"In the second apparition, some things were repeated that were also repeated in the course of subsequent apparitions," Fr. Valinho explained. "One phenomenon concerned the visionaries. At a certain point in this second apparition, they felt once again as if they were enveloped in a light that shone from the lady.

"Within that light, they felt they were able to grasp some very important spiritual truths. On different occasions Lucia has said that the light that penetrated them was so strong that neither she nor Francisco nor Jacinta were able to keep their eyes fixed on the apparition. They had to keep looking down because they felt as though they were being blinded."

"How did Our Lady appear to the children? Until now, you have spoken to us about intense light. Did Lucia give any other details on how she looked?" we asked Fr. Valinho.

"In general, when Lucia has described the apparitions, she has always spoken about light, intense light that was stronger than the sun, and about a very beautiful lady. Even Jacinta said that she was a very beautiful woman—the most beautiful woman that you can imagine. People who questioned her about this pointed to a beautiful young girl in their presence and asked her, 'Is she as beautiful as the lady?'

"She always answered, 'The lady is much more pretty, much more. There is no comparison.'"

"Besides her beauty, what else made an impression on the visionaries?"

"During the various interrogations, especially the one with Monsignor Manuel Nunes Formigão, canon of the Archdiocese of Lisbon, the three children added some interesting details. The canon was very astute. He also asked them questions about the visible aspect of the apparition, and they responded.

"They said that the lady appeared to be about fifteen or sixteen years old. She wore a long white garment that went down to her feet and that was trimmed with a gold border. Her posture was that of a person who was praying. Her hands were folded together at her breast and she held a rosary.

"The canon asked what her hair color was and whether she wore earrings. Jacinta and Francisco said that they couldn't see her hair or her ears because the veil that she was wearing on her head covered them. But Lucia, on the other hand, said that she wore two little rings on her ears, and that on the front of her dress were two gold cords that came down from around her neck to her waist, where they were tied in a gold knot."

"Did anyone try to draw the lady based on this information?"

"After Church authorities recognized the authenticity of the apparitions, some statues were made according to Lucia's directions. The best is one that was made by Giuseppe Terdin. He was able to speak with Sr. Lucia at length in order to know exactly the expression on Mary's face and the correct position of her hands.

"When his work was completed, Sr. Lucia was asked whether the Virgin Mary really did appear as she did in the statue. She answered that a comparison was not entirely possible, but that among all the representations of Mary that she had seen, this was the one that was least ugly. The statue is in the chapel of the Carmel in Coimbra, the cloister where my aunt is living."

A Dreamlike Atmosphere

"There is another extremely interesting phenomenon that was observed by those present," Fr. Valinho continued, "and that was repeated each time thereafter. It was a change in the lighting around the countryside during the mysterious encounter."

"In what sense?"

"When Lucia said, 'There, the Madonna is coming,' my aunt saw very strong flashes of light. They warned her that the apparition was imminent. The people looked around, looked at the little oak tree, and checked the sky, hoping to see something. There were many people who testified at each apparition that they noticed some notable yet inexplicable things.

"Some people saw a ball of light cross the sky and settle upon the oak tree. Monsignor João Quaresma, the vicar general of the diocese of Leiria, has left us his written testimony in this regard. He attended an apparition with another monsignor, Manuel do Carmo Gois, so that he could observe everything that happened. Afterwards the two monsignors testified that they had seen 'a luminous ball that moved from east to west slowly and majestically through the sky.'

"Others saw a little white cloud that descended from the sky and positioned itself upon the oak tree. It remained there throughout the apparition and then floated away. During the apparitions people also noticed that the light from the sun suddenly diminished and that a light breeze was blowing in the area around Cova da Iria.

"The countryside changed color, as did the faces of the people. Everything was bathed in a strange glow that permeated them with the colors of the rainbow. It was as if they had entered a dreamlike environment, a fantasy land."

"How long did these strange things last?"

"The phenomenon lasted until Lucia told the people that the Blessed Mother was leaving. Then everyone heard a powerful clap of thunder, like an explosion, and the rumble of an earthquake. It struck fear in their hearts. Sometimes it was so strong that many people ran away because they were scared."

Like the Buzzing of Bees

"It was really a very impressive phenomenon," we commented.

"People really discussed it a lot," Fr. Valinho concurred. "It has been said that people were strongly influenced by Lucia's words. Maybe. But it's strange that the phenomenon happened every time, at every apparition, and that thousands and thousands of people noticed it.

"Moreover, those who were close to the oak tree during the apparitions perceived and observed some very interesting and curious things. For example, they saw the little branches of the tree, which were strong and rigid, bend as though someone were 'stepping on' them. They also said that they distinctly heard Lucia's words and immediately afterwards perceived a faint noise come from the oak tree, like the buzzing of bees. My Uncle Manuel and my mother have confirmed this faint noise, like the buzzing of bees."

"What do these things mean?"

"It's difficult to give any interpretation. Maybe the Blessed Virgin wanted other people to sense her presence. Or you could reflect on the fact that Mary is in heaven in body and in soul. It's certainly a 'glorified body,' but we don't understand very well what the word 'glorified' means. Since we know that a body is made of matter, maybe she wanted to leave some trace of her movement. Maybe!

"These are little details that can help us sense the greatness and the beauty of the dogma of the Assumption, and, at the same time, the beauty of the reality that awaits us all, the resurrection of our bodies as Christ promised, which is almost inconceivable to our poor minds."

Francisco's Questions

"But let's get back to the facts," Fr. Valinho said. "So it was during this second apparition that the Virgin Mary prophesied that Francisco and Jacinta would die at an early age and that Lucia would live for a long time. In the first apparition, Our Lady, in responding specifically to one of Lucia's questions, had said that the three children would all go to heaven. This time, at the request of her two cousins, Lucia once again asked to go to heaven, and Our Lady specifically said that Francisco and Jacinta would die soon, while Lucia would remain on this earth to spread devotion to the Immaculate Heart of Mary."

"And the light that Sr. Lucia spoke about?"

"Only later did Lucia reveal that, as soon as she said these words,

Mary parted her hands, and the reflection of the intense light in which she was enveloped penetrated the three children, just as it had done in the first apparition. Once again the three children had that wonderful mystical experience which I have already described. They felt as if they were immersed in God.

"Lucia added that two beams of light came from Mary's hands: one descended towards the earth, and the other went up to the sky. She said it seemed to her that she saw Jacinta and Francisco in the ray of light that went up to the sky, while she saw herself in the one that descended to the earth. It must have made a strong impression on her because later, when she was in the Carmel in Coimbra, my aunt wanted to have a statue of Mary sculpted in this position."

"So this time Lucia was also the only one who spoke."

"That's right. Lucia was the only one who spoke, just as she was the only one to speak during the apparitions of the angel and the other apparitions of the Virgin. Jacinta saw Mary and heard her voice, but Francisco only saw her. He saw the lady's lips moving, but he didn't hear her voice.

"Therefore, he wanted to know what Mary had said, and he reflected on Lucia's responses. Then he asked other questions so that he might better understand. Francisco demonstrated that he was a very thoughtful child, one who asked questions.

" 'Why did Mary have a heart crowned with thorns in her hand?' Francisco asked Lucia. 'Why did she shine God's great light on the earth? Why were you in the light that came down to the earth while Jacinta and I were in the light that went up to the sky?'

" 'It's because you and Jacinta will soon go to heaven, while I'll remain for a good while here on earth to spread devotion to the Immaculate Heart of Mary.'

" 'How many years will you stay here?'

" 'I don't know. Several.'

" 'Did Mary tell you that?'

" 'Yes, and I saw it in that light that she put on our hearts.' "

"Confess That You've Lied"

The fifty people who were present at the second apparition partly consisted of those who were simply curious, but there were also a good number of people there who knew the children well and did not think they were lying. They returned home enthusiastic and convinced that the whole thing was both serious and credible. They began to share their impressions with others, telling their neighbors about their experience. Interest and curiosity increased, as well as hostility from those who did not believe. Skeptics made fun of the three children with much more force.

"Look, Lucia," they said, pointing their finger up at the sky. "There's a lady walking over people's heads."

Or they threatened them by saying, "You could use a good spanking," or, "If you were my children, I'd make that tale of the visions go away."

In Fatima and in the surrounding countryside, people could not talk about anything else. People were divided down the middle. The parish priest was worried. He told the Marto family and the dos Santos family that he wanted to question the children.

Manuel Marto, who fiercely defended his children, went immediately to see the priest. "My children are little," he said. "I don't want them to be scared or upset by any interrogations."

The priest tried to calm him down, and even appeared understanding. He said he only wanted to know what was going on. Since people were talking about visions and apparitions, he felt it was his duty to try to understand. Manuel Marto told him that he personally would accompany his children to the parish the following day.

"On the other hand, my grandmother, Maria Rosa, Lucia's mother, was thrilled to hear about the summons," Fr. Valinho recalled. "She couldn't believe that the parish priest was going to intervene. Because of his authority, she thought that he would be able to convince her daughter that she should confess that she made everything up.

" 'Tomorrow we'll go to the early morning Mass,' she told Lucia. 'Then you'll go to see the pastor. I hope he makes you confess the truth.' "

"What did Lucia think at the time?" we asked Fr. Valinho.

"Sr. Lucia told me that she was very afraid that morning, especially since her sisters, including my mother, kept telling her that she really would be scolded. The whole family hoped that the priest would be able to convince her that she should confess that she was lying.

"That evening she went to see Francisco and Jacinta. 'We'll go with you,' her cousins told her. 'If he beats us, we'll suffer together for the conversion of sinners.' "

"So the much-feared day arrived ..."

"Yes. In the morning my grandmother accompanied Lucia to the church. Along the way, my grandmother didn't say a word, and Lucia remembers this little detail to this day. She suffered greatly when she saw that her mother was so suspicious, so indifferent, and so convinced that her daughter was a liar. 'I have to confess that I was shaking as I thought of everything that could happen,' she told me more than once.

"When Mass was over, they went up to the priest's house. At the foot of the stairs my grandmother turned to her and said, 'Now don't annoy me any more! Confess to the pastor that you lied, so that he can tell people next Sunday that it was a lie. After that, it will be finished. What nonsense! To make people run all the way to Cova da Iria to pray before a tree?'

"Francisco and Jacinta also went to see the priest. He first questioned Jacinta, who didn't say a word since she was mindful of how much she had made Lucia suffer with her earlier indiscretions. She just looked down and was quiet as a fish. Francisco responded the same way.

"Lucia, on the other hand, told everything that had happened. She confirmed without any hesitation that they had seen the beautiful lady two times and had promised to return to Cova da Iria on the thirteenth day of each month until October."

"What was the priest's reaction?" we asked curiously.

"Sr. Lucia told me that he was pleasant and understanding. But at the end of the meeting, when he was speaking with the children's parents, he told them that he was perplexed. He said that, from all he was able to learn, there was nothing supernatural.

" 'It doesn't seem possible,' he said, 'that Mary would come down from heaven only to say that people should pray the rosary every day. It's something most of our families already do. Moreover, we know from the accounts of other apparitions that our Lord or the Blessed Mother generally tells the souls to whom they appear that they should tell everything to their pastor or confessor. In this case, though, the children refuse to speak to me.

" 'I'm afraid that the devil is tricking them,' he solemnly ruled. After a long silence, he added, 'It wouldn't be the first time. Satan takes advantage of every occasion to sow confusion. Satan even takes possession of holy people, approaches the altar, and even takes Communion in an effort to sow lies and confusion among the faithful.

" 'Nonetheless, we shouldn't make any hasty judgments. We have to wait and see what happens over time.' "

"Were the children aware of such a serious judgment?"

"The children were present and heard everything. They listened to the pastor's final statement with consternation. His words about Satan stirred a feeling of disgust and fear in them.

"Overall, though, they were happy with how things went. They had not been punished as they had feared, and the priest was kind to them. My grandmother, on the other hand, was not very pleased. She had hoped that he would resolve such an intricate matter, but nothing happened."

11

IN HELL'S FIRE

"What if the priest is right?" Lucia began to ask herself.

Her pastor's allusion to the devil frightened her. The priest's words were constantly spinning in her head and troubled her. Lucia knew her catechism well, and even before her first Communion she had learned that Satan was both God's and humanity's avowed enemy. He was always setting traps to lead souls to eternal damnation.

She remembered that the priest had said in a sermon that the devil's presence always sowed confusion, disorder, worries, rebellion, and war. She also reflected on the fact that ever since the apparitions had begun, peace and tranquillity had disappeared from her family's life. Before, there had always been harmony and happiness. Now, sadness, sickness, and tears reigned.

Even the atmosphere in the village had changed. The apparitions had become a source of division and had pitted members of the same family against one another. "If Satan really brings war and division," Lucia said to herself, "then Satan is the one who is appearing to us at Cova da Iria. The priest is right."

The doubt was overwhelming. She felt ashamed whenever she thought about what her pastor had said. Yet it seemed to make sense in light of everything that was happening.

As she reflected on this thought, painful as it was, the visions of the angel kept coming to mind, as well as the joy that she had experienced at those times. She also recalled the deep emotion that the unforgettable beauty of the lady stirred up in her heart. Then she wondered, "How could all these beautiful and healthy feelings be caused by the devil?"

She could hear her pastor's voice as he sharply said, "Satan even takes possession of the bodies of saintly people at times. Satan even comes to the altar to take Communion."

She was upset and even trembled upon hearing these words. Every time she thought about them, she experienced disgust and fear. She had to be cautious and ask the Lord to free her from any influence of the devil. But the agony had taken its toll, and it was difficult to pray.

Was It All a Trick?

"Why are you so sad?" Jacinta asked her.

"I was thinking about what the priest said," Lucia answered absentmindedly.

"He said that we have to wait and not rush in making a judgment."

"But he also said that it could be the devil's influence."

"That's not the devil," Jacinta retorted sharply. "The devil is very ugly, and the lady is beautiful. The devil lives under the earth, in hell, and we saw the lady going up to heaven."

Lucia smiled. Jacinta was just a little girl. She could not even conceive of the possibility that the devil was deceiving them.

But she herself was beginning to feel that it was all Satan's work. She knew that her mother was very religious, and faithful to the Church. So she knew that her mother could be right and sensed danger.

How could she have thought that Mary would come down from heaven and appear to her, a poor shepherd girl, especially with all the holy people throughout the world? Yes, the priest was right.

Everything that was happening was one of Satan's tricks.

Then she had a nightmare that confirmed her feelings. Lucia's mother had taught her that dreams are important. Everyone in Fatima believed in dreams. They thought that they were premonitions or warnings of what could happen.

"I saw the devil laughing because he had deceived me, and he was trying to drag me into hell," Lucia wrote in her memoirs. "Seeing myself in his clutches, I began to call on Mary, shouting so loud that I woke up my mother, who was worried and woke me up.

"That night, I couldn't fall asleep because I was paralyzed with fear. That dream left a cloud of real fear and worry in my spirit. Relief came only when I was alone, where I could cry my heart out. I even began to feel annoyed by my cousins' company."

Time went by. Life went on as usual. The three children took the sheep out to pasture every day. But their days were no longer as peaceful.

They continued to pray, but not with the same enthusiasm as before. Lucia, with her doubts, was upset. She had changed. She said very little, avoided her cousins, and was irritable and rude. Francisco and Jacinta suffered when they saw her in this state, and wept.

They did not stop offering sacrifices and prayers to the Lord. Lucia participated, but without enthusiasm. "During those months," she wrote in her memoirs, "I lost my enthusiasm for offering sacrifices and for mortification. I was doubtful, trying to decide whether I should say that I had lied to end the whole thing once and for all."

"The Little Saint of Rotten Wood"

As July 13 drew near, Lucia's inner struggle grew stronger. Finally, she made up her mind. "Let Jacinta and Francisco go if they want to. I shall not go any more to Cova da Iria."

The evening of July 12 seemed like a holiday in Fatima. It was a Thursday, a normal weekday. Yet an unusually large number of strangers were milling around town, as if there were a fair.

They had come for the apparition on the following day. Many asked where the visionaries lived, so they could satisfy their curiosity. People who were sick had also come.

Lucia was worried as she watched this activity, and thought her mother was right. "I'm the one who caused all this," she said. "And if it's a trick of the devil, I'm responsible for the problems it will cause."

As nightfall approached, she went to Francisco and Jacinta's house.

"I'm not going tomorrow to Cova da Iria," Lucia said.

"Why not?" the two children asked with a stunned and sad look.

"I think the priest is right. It can be the devil's influence."

"That's not possible," Jacinta protested strongly.

"I wish it were so, but I feel otherwise."

Jacinta began to cry.

"We'll still go," Francisco said. "The lady has made an appointment with us, and we cannot miss it."

Lucia hugged them and returned to her house. When she saw that a crowd of people was waiting for her outside, she hid in some bushes next to the well, where she could find some relief from her sorrow in silence.

She returned to her home only when it was dark and the curious had left. Her mother thought that she had stayed out to play and greeted her sarcastically, "There's our little girl! A little saint of rotten wood! After tending the sheep, she spends all her time playing so that no one will find her."

Lucia was hurt by her sarcasm, but she did not say a word. She thought she deserved her mother's scorn, as well as the scorn of everyone else in the village. She had let Satan trick her and had caused a lot of confusion for many people who had believed in her.

She slept fitfully all night long. Every so often she would suddenly wake up and start to cry.

In the morning she woke up early and took the sheep to pasture. It was already the hot season. She decided she would return by nine o'clock and hide so that she could spend the rest of the day far away from everyone.

She did not know what to say when she saw her cousins. Their eyes were red, and she knew that they had been crying. She felt sad. She also felt responsible. She was the oldest, and she should have understood from the beginning that she should not have let things go this far.

She was silent for the whole time. Every little while Jacinta raised her arms up to heaven and invited her friends to pray. Lucia joined them, but without any conviction.

When the sun began to heat up the countryside, they gathered the sheep and returned home.

"You're not going to Cova da Iria?" Jacinta asked sheepishly.

"I already told you last night," Lucia answered abruptly. "I'm not going there anymore." Hastily she walked away.

She put the sheep in their pen and hid in some bushes to avoid the curiosity of the people who were gathered in front of her house. Her heart was full of grief and confusion. She wanted to pray but was unable to do so. She found comfort in her tears.

Around eleven o'clock, she suddenly felt different. She felt a strong force pulling her out of her hiding place and urging her to go to Cova da Iria. At once her doubts and worries disappeared. Once again Lucia felt an indescribable urge to see the lady who was brighter than the sun.

She was sitting in front of a bush. She jumped to her feet and said to herself, "I have to go. I'm already late. Mary is calling me." She had a clear conviction that all her suffering and doubts were caused by the devil, who wanted to prevent her from seeing the lady. Satan's real plan was to keep her away from the Blessed Virgin.

Lucia went straight to her cousins' house. Jacinta and Francisco were in their room crying.

"So you're not going to Cova da Iria?" Lucia asked.

The two cousins looked at her in astonishment.

"We didn't have the courage to go without you," Jacinta said timidly. "You're the one who always spoke with the lady, and we don't know how to."

"Come on, Lucia, let's go to Cova da Iria," Francisco begged.

"I'm going with you," Lucia said. Her face was radiant.

Jacinta and Francisco could not believe their ears. They hugged and kissed their cousin. Lucia was her usual self—happy and sure of herself.

"We love you so much," Jacinta told her with tears in her eyes.

"Get ready, my little one. We're late," Lucia answered.

"We Have to Protect Them"

Within a few minutes, all three of them were walking out of the house. Olimpia watched them in silence.

"Mama, we're going to Cova da Iria," Jacinta said as she waved goodbye.

"Don't forget, be careful. There are many people," Olimpia murmured.

She stood at the door, following the three children with her gaze. She felt a pain in her heart at the sight of so many strangers in the street, and she was overwhelmed by a sudden sense of fear. She decided to consult with Maria Rosa, Lucia's mother. She put a thin shawl over her shoulders and went to her house.

Maria Rosa was in the kitchen, and she, too, looked tense and worried.

"I fear for our children," Olimpia said. "All those people! Who knows what could happen there!"

"If they truly see Mary, she'll protect them," Maria Rosa said, pretending to be peaceful. "But if it's not true, I don't know what could happen," she quickly added. "An angry crowd could really do them harm. Let's go. We have to protect them."

She, too, put on a shawl so that no one would recognize her, and the two women went quickly down the road to Cova da Iria.

Manuel Marto was in the fields near his house. He had just finished working, and he, too, watched anxiously and incredulously as so many strangers walked down the road. He never could have imagined that so many people would come to Fatima. He, too, began to think about the harm some could do to the children—especially Jacinta, who was so little. He dropped his hoe and started down the road.

It seemed as if there were a big country fair at Cova da Iria. Glancing around, Manuel calculated that there were no fewer than four thousand people there. He stood on a little hill from which he could see the whole area, which was shaped like an amphitheater. The children were down there, next to the little oak tree, over which Mary supposedly appeared.

Manuel Marto decided to get closer, but he was unable to do so. Everyone was crowded around the visionaries. They wanted to be as close as possible to the place of the apparitions, hoping to see something. So Manuel found a big rock from which he could keep an eye on his children. He sat down and did not take his eyes off them.

Some adults, who were protecting them from the crowd, surrounded Lucia, Francisco, and Jacinta. He recognized two farmers, two men who were strong and imposing. One was a former policeman.

"They're in good hands," Manuel Marto thought, a little relieved. But he continued to watch them worriedly. "It seemed like chaos," he recalled when he was already an old man.

The former policeman spotted him and signaled him to come closer.

"I can't," Manuel answered, making signs with his hands.

"Stand back," the policeman cried with a commanding voice. "Stand back. That's the children's father. Let him through."

His imposing figure struck fear, and his voice, reverence. People stepped back immediately, creating a pathway. Marto, a little embarrassed, joined the three children. He stood next to Jacinta, whom he hugged affectionately.

Lucia knelt down and began to pray the rosary. Everyone imitated her. Her childish voice echoed through the valley. The crowd listened to the first part of the Hail Mary in dead silence and responded in chorus.

When the rosary was over, Lucia stood up. "There, I saw the flash of lightning. Mary's coming," she cried.

The sun darkened a little, and a light breeze began to blow. The crowd was silent.

The lady who was brighter than the sun was there once again, before the three children.

The Blessed Virgin said, "I want you to come here on the thirteenth of next month. I want you to continue to pray the rosary every day in honor of Our Lady of the Rosary with the intention of obtaining peace in the world and an end to the war, because she alone can help you."

"I wish to ask you to tell us who you are and to perform a miracle so that everyone believes that you did appear," Lucia said.

Her request was rooted in the anguish that she had experienced during the last few days, which stemmed from her doubts that the beautiful woman might be a diabolical illusion. Mary understood and reassured her, saying, "Continue to come here every month. In October I will tell you who I am and what I desire, and I shall perform a great miracle so that the whole world may see and believe you."

She paused and then said, "Make sacrifices for sinners and say often, especially when you are making some sacrifices: 'O Jesus, it is out of love for you, for the conversion of sinners, and as reparation for the offenses against the Immaculate Heart of Mary.' "

Once again she stretched out her hands as she had done in previous months.

A Horrible Vision

"Then we saw what looked like a great sea of fire," Sr. Lucia wrote in her memoirs, "that seemed to be under the earth. In this sea of fire were plunged, black and burning, demons and souls with a human form, resembling live transparent coals. Lifted up into the air by the flames, they fell back on all sides like sparks in a conflagration, with neither weight nor balance, amid loud screams and cries of pain and despair that made one tremble and shudder with terror. The demons were distinguished from human beings by their horrible, disgusting animal forms, known to us but transparent as live coals. The vision lasted a moment.

"We were scared, and as if asking for help, we raised our eyes to the Blessed Virgin. With kindness and sadness she said, 'You have seen hell, and the souls of poor sinners. To save them, Our Lord wishes to establish in the world devotion to my Immaculate Heart.

" 'If people will do what I shall tell you, many souls will be saved and there will be peace in the world. The war is coming to an end, but if the offenses against God do not cease, under the pontificate of Pius XI a still more terrible one will begin. When you see the night sky illuminated by an unfamiliar light, you will know that it is the important sign that God is giving you before punishing the world for its crimes, by means of war, famine, and persecution of the Church and the Holy Father.

" 'To prevent it, I shall come to ask for the consecration of Russia to my Immaculate Heart and the Communion of reparation on the first Saturday of the month. If you honor my request, Russia will be converted and there will be peace. If not, Russia will spread its errors throughout the world, provoking wars and persecution against the Church. Many good people will be martyred, the Holy Father will have to suffer much, and many nations will be destroyed.

" 'In the end, my Immaculate Heart will triumph. The Holy Father will consecrate Russia to me. Russia will be converted, and a time of peace will be given to the world. The dogma of the faith will always be maintained in Portugal ...'"

At this point, Sr. Lucia's manuscript is interrupted. The dots indicate that she left out the rest of Mary's words. It was that part of the secret, known as the "third secret of Fatima," that has not yet been revealed.

Then Lucia once again quotes the Virgin. "Don't tell this [that is, the part to be kept secret] to anyone, except Francisco. When you pray the rosary, after each decade say, 'O my Jesus, forgive us our sins and save us from the fires of hell. Lead all souls to heaven, especially those that most need your mercy.'

" 'Do you not want any more from me?' I asked.

" 'No. There is nothing more I want from you today.'

"And as usual, she began to rise up to the east until she disappeared in the immensity of the firmament."

This is Sr. Lucia's written account. Eyewitnesses say that they heard a strong clap of thunder at this moment. Two lanterns were hanging from an arch that had been constructed near the little oak tree. The lanterns began to shake as if there were an earthquake. Many people swore that they saw a little cloud of light over the oak tree during the apparition, and that they heard a buzzing sound coming from the cloud, like the noise from a hornets' nest.

When the apparition was over, people approached the three children. Everyone was asking questions.

"Lucia, what did the Virgin Mary say?"

"Many things."

"At one point we heard you cry out in fright. Why?"

"I can't tell you. It's a secret."

"A secret?"

"Yes, something I can't tell you."

"Good or bad?"

"Good for some, bad for others."

"When will you tell it to us?"

"I don't know."

The word "secret" aroused curiosity. People pressed around them wanting to know. They were suffocating the children. Manuel Marto was worried. He took Jacinta in his arms, held her tightly to him, and elbowed his way to the path. Behind him the ex-policeman had taken Francisco in his arms and put him on his shoulders. Lucia followed him, surrounded by her friends.

12

THE SECRET

Lucia's use of the word "secret" after the July 13 apparition piqued the curiosity of many people.

"What could the secret be?" the people of Fatima asked. People in neighboring towns also raised the same question. Every day people stopped by the homes of the little shepherd children and asked to speak with them. Rich, elegantly dressed women in enormous automobiles even came from Lisbon. Everyone wanted to know the secret.

The three visionaries began to feel as though people were hounding them, tailing them, and checking up on them. When they would come home with their sheep, they carefully scrutinized the road ahead. If they saw an unfamiliar face, they hid.

Often the visitors were very pushy. They would visit the children's homes during dinnertime, since they were certain that they would find the children there.

People sought out Jacinta the most. People assumed she would be the one most ready to talk, since she was the youngest. Women took her in their arms, gave her gifts, and promised to give her money in exchange for the secret. But Jacinta, remembering everything that had happened when she had spoken out after the first apparition, always responded with silence.

The secret even made the pastor of the parish in Fatima suspicious. Although he had already met with the three children, he wanted to meet with them again.

He realized that this latest apparition had made a strong impression on the people who had been present. Many had heard Lucia's sad moan during the vision and had seen the expression of terror on her face. What they had seen and heard remained vivid in their minds. Moreover, nobody could forget the clap of thunder at the end, which seemed so threatening.

The pastor of the parish also wanted to know the secret. He interrogated the visionaries one by one, but he could not get a word out of them.

"What Mary revealed to the visionaries during her third apparition at Cova da Iria is of fundamental importance," Fr. Valinho said. "The Virgin Mary drew the children's attention, and through them the attention of all men and women, to the eternal history of humanity and the supreme destiny of each person, which is linked to the forces of good and evil. These are truths that we have already spoken about, which are contained in the traditional doctrine of the Church.

"But people often neglect or forget these truths in their teaching, so these truths often do not have the right effect. Obviously Mary wanted the people of God to pay attention to them once again, especially in the coming years, when these truths would be even more neglected and questioned. This is perhaps why she asked the three visionaries not to reveal at that moment everything she told them. This is the reason for the secret."

"God Doesn't Like to Shock People"

We stood in the large piazza in front of the shrine, as we waited for Fr. Valinho to take us to a place called Valinhos. There, the fourth apparition took place. Before leaving, Fr. Valinho wanted to stop and reflect on the message of the third apparition.

"That day," he told us, "Mary gave the children the essence of her message. But when people talk about it in a superficial way and describe the vision as if it were a scene from a movie, as people generally do, they end up distorting the truth contained therein. It's a message that we have to ponder from a theological point of view. Only then will we understand its value and its importance for today."

In the last chapter, we reconstructed the events that occurred on July 13, 1917, based on the facts as we now know them. That account included a part of the vision that Mary asked to be kept secret, which Lucia only described in detail some time later when the Virgin Mary told her to do so. Therefore, we now know everything that happened. So Fr. Valinho explained the meaning that we should attach to that apparition.

"But why did Mary confide such important things to the three visionaries and ask them not to tell anyone?" we asked Fr. Valinho. "Why did the Virgin Mary give Lucia permission to make these secrets public only many years afterwards?"

"The reasons certainly are there; otherwise, Mary would not have given such orders to the visionaries," Fr. Valinho explained patiently. "But we don't know what they are. Perhaps the Blessed Virgin didn't want people to speculate on such important matters.

"If the children had immediately revealed their vision of hell, there would have been no end to the laughter. The press, especially in Portugal, was in the hands of the anticlerics and the Masons. To speak openly of such a matter might have been more harmful than helpful.

"Then too, discretion is the typical style in spiritual matters. God doesn't like to shock people or assert himself in a sensational way. He gives us little hints so we can reflect on them, get our bearings, and freely make our choice."

An Infinite Mystery

"In order to understand the importance of the Blessed Virgin's revelations," Fr. Valinho explained, "we have to digress a little and recall some fundamental points. Catholic doctrine teaches us that man was given a unique gift: a free will. At every point in his existence, he can choose between good and evil.

"Man, however, has abused this unique gift from the beginning. Adam, the first man, whom God put in Paradise on earth, gave in to Satan and rebelled against his Creator. But God, in his infinite goodness, wanted to 'stand in the gap' by sending his own Son, Jesus, the New Adam, who was sacrificed for the redemption of the world.

"He restored man's dignity and his stature as a son of God. But man is still weak and fragile. Jesus, Mary, the angels, and the saints are constantly helping individuals on the road to salvation, even through extraordinary interventions such as apparitions. The Blessed Virgin especially acts in this way since she, our mother, knows better than anyone the difficulties that her children face."

"So this is the deeper meaning of the events at Fatima?"

"Exactly. Mary came to Fatima to bring extraordinary help for the umpteenth time. Once again she wanted to draw our attention to the biggest danger that we face. It is the same old enemy, Satan, a murderer from the very beginning, the instigator of all evil, who is intent on leading as many people as possible to eternal damnation.

"The Virgin has denounced Satan as the author of mortal destruction, of horrible deceit, and of dreadful consequences. She has offered herself as a weapon of salvation and secure help against such an enemy. She has indicated that, because God wills it, her Immaculate Heart is the inexhaustible source of indispensable energy for winning the ultimate battle. This is the message of Fatima."

"The famous secret contains all this?"

"Even more. I've summarized it, but Lucia has told us that the secret consists of three parts. The first refers to the vision of hell; the second refers to devotion to the Immaculate Heart of Mary; the third part is still unknown. This third part continues to arouse the world's curiosity. Hundreds of books and thousands of articles have been written about the contents of this third part, but it is still unknown."

The Pope Knows Everything

"Yet the first and the second parts were revealed many years later," we observed.

"Mary asked Lucia not to say anything to anyone, except to Francisco, who had seen but had not heard what she said. Many years later, when she was told to do so from heaven, Lucia revealed that secret. She revealed the first and second parts to everyone, but she revealed the third part only to the pope, who was Pope Pius XII at the time.

"Furthermore, she sent the third part of the secret to the pope accompanied by a letter in which she told him that he could reveal Mary's prophetic words whenever he felt it opportune to do so, but only after 1960. But no pope has yet made the decision to do so."

"When you were referring to Lucia, why did you say, 'When she was told to do so from heaven?' "

"Because this is what Lucia herself said. She decided to speak only when she was told to speak."

"This can lead us to believe that the Blessed Mother appeared to Lucia on other occasions after the apparitions in 1917."

"That's exactly the case. My aunt has continued to have 'encounters' with the Blessed Virgin. She has explicitly mentioned some of them in her memoirs."

"When did Lucia receive orders to reveal the secret that she had received in July of 1917?"

"In 1927. The Blessed Virgin appeared to her while she was praying in the chapel of the novitiate in Tuy, Spain, and told her that she could reveal the first two parts of the secret. Lucia spoke with her confessor, who told her to write everything down, but it seems that he then gave her back the pages she had written without even reading them.

"Later on, Lucia revealed the contents of those two parts of the secret to two Jesuits, the provincial superior of the Sisters of St. Dorothy and the bishop of Leiria. By the end of 1927, these people were aware of certain facts that would occur just as predicted during the century, such as World War II, which was preceded by the famous aurora borealis, and the sad events in Russia."

An Uncomfortable Truth

"Why didn't Lucia's confessor and the other people to whom she had revealed the secret pay much attention to what she was saying?"

"The Church had not yet made any judgment on the authenticity of the apparitions, so priests were very prudent and on their guard. This always happens. The Church never rushes to make a judgment.

"So after the apparitions in Fatima, Church authorities had continued their hearings, studies, and examinations, and it was only in 1930 that they concluded they were genuine. On October 31 of that year, the bishop sent out a pastoral letter declaring that 'the visions of the shepherd children were worthy of faith' and 'officially permitting the cult of Our Lady of Fatima.' It was the beginning of a new era in the history of Fatima.

"The decision was made to build a large shrine. The bishop then began to ask Lucia to write down everything she remembered, in order to have ample documentation. Lucia sent him the first volume of her memoirs on Christmas Day of 1935, and the second one two years later.

"Meanwhile, a book about Jacinta was going to be published, and the bishop asked her for some further clarifications. It was then that Lucia sent a detailed memoir on the two parts of the secret as well. This time it was published."

"The first part of the secret concerns the vision of hell," we noted. "When it was revealed, it was widely criticized, especially by some illustrious theologians who said that it was an anachronistic vision connected to old traditions, and that it was not based on precise theological truths."

"Yes, there was a lot of criticism. Hell is not a popular truth, so people tend to gloss over it. But it is a choice that man makes by rejecting the truth that has been revealed to him.

"Undoubtedly the devil is behind such a choice, but man remains responsible for it. We don't know how and when such a choice leads him to eternal damnation. We don't know how many people are lost. But the fact is that this reality exists."

"In the first two parts of the secret that Lucia revealed," we observed, playing the role of the devil's advocate, "there are explicit references to historic facts that did indeed occur. Knowing that Lucia received these secrets in 1917, we can't help but be surprised by the fact that Mary used names that Lucia could not know at the time and that no one would have understood back then.

"For example, Mary said, 'The war is coming to an end, but if the offenses against God do not cease, during the pontificate of Pius XI a still more terrible one will begin.' It might have been easy to predict that World War I was about to end. But to say back in 1917 that another one would begin under Pius XI really sounds unbelievable.

"Back then Pope Benedict XV was the pope. Was she sure that Mary did mention the name of Pius XI, who would only be elected five years later? Or did Lucia insert that name later, when she was writing her memoirs?"

"Sr. Lucia has always said categorically that Mary explicitly mentioned Pius XI. Someone pointed out to her that the war actually began under Pius XII. She answered that Germany carried out the first act of war when its troops invaded Austria during the night of March 11-12, 1938. Hitler arrested the chancellor of Austria, Kurt von Schuschnigg, and two days later, on March 15, he announced the annexation of Austria, which then became a province in the Third Reich.

"Lucia also indicated a sign that would appear in the sky to announce the impending war, 'a night illuminated by an unfamiliar light.' On the night of January 24-25, 1938, the sky over Europe was illuminated by a mysterious and disturbing glimmer. Astronomers said that it was simply the aurora borealis. Lucia, on the other hand, said that it was the sign that Mary had spoken about in 1917. The invasion of Austria and the aurora borealis occurred in 1938, which was during the pontificate of Pius XI, who died on February 10, 1939."

Guilty of Believing

"When recounting the apparition of July 13, 1917," we pointed out, "Lucia said that Mary spoke about Russia. The Blessed Virgin told her that she would return and 'ask for the consecration of Russia to [her] Immaculate Heart and a Communion of reparation on the first Saturday of each month,' in order to avoid war.

"Then she said, 'If people heed my requests, Russia will be converted. If they are not, Russia will spread its errors throughout the world, provoking wars and persecution against the Church. Many good people will be martyred, and many nations will be annihilated.' These are very detailed prophecies, but is it certain that back then, in 1917, Mary explicitly mentioned Russia by name?"

"Naturally people have asked Sr. Lucia many times about this, and she has always answered that she was certain that Mary mentioned Russia by name. In 1917, she was ten years old and had not yet gone to school.

" 'I had heard people talk about the French and the Spanish, but I wasn't familiar with other nations,' she said. 'I certainly know very well that, during the apparition of July, 1917, our Lady explicitly mentioned Russia by name.' Back then, the Bolshevik Revolution, which brought the communists to power, had not yet taken place in Russia. Lucia, a ten-year-old child, couldn't have known about Marxism.

"Even in 1927, when that particular secret was revealed, she could not have imagined that there would be tremendous 'persecution of the Church' in the name of that particular ideology, that 'various nations [would] be annihilated,' and that 'many good people [would] be martyred.' Today we know this ideology, which Pius XI declared to be 'the greatest heresy of all times,' not only spread throughout the world, causing hate and revolutions. From a political point of view, it was a bankrupt system that led to the social and economic ruin of many nations. We also know that it sowed bloodshed and death.

"Solzhenitsyn has written that the communist regime killed sixty-five million people because of their religious faith. Based on recent documents from the Kremlin, the number of victims is considered to be much larger, ranging from eighty million to a hundred or even a hundred and fifty million people. Mary foresaw all this in 1917."

Not What She Asked For

"The Blessed Virgin had said to Lucia, 'I shall come to ask the consecration of Russia to my Immaculate Heart.' Did she return with this request?"

"Certainly. Lucia has said that Mary came and made this request on two occasions. The first time was on December 10, 1925. Lucia was in her room in Tuy, where she was praying.

"Mary appeared to her holding Baby Jesus in her arms and said, 'Look, my daughter, at my heart. It is surrounded with thorns because men have pierced it every minute of the day with their blasphemy and ingratitude. You, at least, are trying to console me by practicing the first Saturdays of the month.'

"Mary said that she would ask people to practice the devotion of the first Saturdays of the month. This, along with the consecration of Russia to the Immaculate Heart of Mary, would serve as a means of avoiding war, persecution, and massacres. Lucia tried to spread this devotion by speaking with her bishop and with people whom she knew. She even invited her mother to observe this practice, as documented in a letter she wrote on July 24, 1927. Mary returned to ask explicitly for the consecration of Russia when she appeared to Lucia in 1929."

"Was this consecration done?"

"Lucia told her confessor, her bishop, her superior, and some priests whom she knew, and she even wrote to Pope Pius XII in 1940. She said that Mary's exact wish was that the Holy Father would perform the consecration of Russia to the Immaculate Heart of Mary. She also ordered that all the Catholic bishops of the world perform it at the same time in union with the Holy Father. However, this unity was lacking, and the consecration wasn't done."

"Nevertheless, John Paul II successfully carried out Mary's request."

"He did so only in 1984, almost sixty years after the request was made. As we have noted, an attempt was made on the pope's life in St. Peter's Square in 1981. He was struck by the fact that this attempt occurred on May 13, the anniversary of Mary's first apparition in Fatima.

"He started to take a special interest in the event, and probably discovered many things and many interesting coincidences. He also reflected on the strange fact that Mary's expressed desire concerning the consecration to Russia was never carried out. He decided to make up for lost time.

"In 1982, the Holy Father went to Fatima to thank the Virgin for having saved his life, as he himself said publicly, and to perform the consecration of Russia from Fatima. In a certain sense, it was a personal initiative. He did not succeed in having the whole Church join him. At that time Lucia said, 'This is not the consecration that Mary asked for.' "

"What happened then?"

"When he returned to Rome, the Pope contacted the bishops throughout the world and finally succeeded in convincing all of them to comply. On December 8, 1983, he sent a letter to all the bishops of the world, asking them to prepare a prayer service for this solemn occasion. He also sent them the act of consecration that he would be praying.

"On March 24, 1984, Pope John Paul II consecrated Russia and the entire world to Mary's care in St. Peter's Basilica in Rome, before a statue of the Blessed Virgin of Fatima that had been brought from Portugal. This time it conformed to the Blessed Virgin's request."

"And the third part of the secret?"

Everyone Wants to Know

"Lucia received permission to reveal it in 1941, but only to the pope. She was at the convent in Tuy, Spain. On June 17 she sent a sealed packet to her own bishop, who, in turn, forwarded it to the Vatican.

"A letter in which Lucia said that Mary had told her that the secret could be revealed only after 1960 accompanied the text of the secret. In 1958 Pope John XXIII ascended the throne of Peter. The following year, he read Lucia's letter but decided not to reveal its contents. Successive popes decided likewise, and we still do not know what Lucia wrote."

"This, in fact, has caused a lot of speculation among many people."

"That's right. Indiscretions, revelations, and inferences began circulating. People were talking about the destruction of the world and nuclear war. People were saying that Pope John XXIII had sent the contents of the secret to the world's leaders, so that people who, in turn, read it then revealed it. In reality, nobody knew anything with certainty. The Church has never taken a position."

"Certainly you have spoken many times with your aunt about this secret. What do you know that others don't?"

"Nothing. My aunt will not budge when it comes to this matter. Several times I tried to bring up the subject to see her reaction, but she immediately changed the subject.

"Nonetheless, she has always tried to make me understand that we have to be optimistic. She has always told me that there is a lot of evil in the world and that Satan is leading many souls to damnation. She always adds, though, that God's goodness and mercy are stronger than any evil, and that his mercy and goodness will triumph in the end."

"Have you formed any kind of personal opinion on the contents of that third part of the secret?"

"Yes, I have my ideas, which, of course, might be totally mistaken. I believe that part of the secret concerns the Church from within, perhaps doctrinal difficulties, a crisis of unity, divisions, or rebellion. The last sentence that my aunt wrote, which precedes the part that is still unknown, says, 'In Portugal the dogma of the faith will always be preserved.' Then the passage that we do not know begins.

"However, we might infer that the subject of the missing part might be related to this last sentence. Therefore, people elsewhere in the Church might waver on dogma. But this is just speculation."

13

THE APPARITION THAT WAS MISSED

The crowd that had gathered at Cova da Iria on July 13 for the Blessed Mother's apparition caused quite a sensation. Four thousand people had endured considerable hardship in order to get to that barren plateau in the Estremadura, which, at that time, was poor and isolated and did not have many roads. Many people had come from distant towns, and some had even come from abroad. News articles had also been published in various newspapers.

Political authorities in the area were concerned about the whole matter. Artur de Oliveira Santos was responsible for the administration of Vila Nova de Ourem, and Fatima was located within his jurisdiction. His position was similar to that of a mayor.

He was fanatically anticlerical and an avowed Mason. He was active in the new political movement in Portugal, which was dedicated to combating any form of religion. When he heard people talking about the alleged apparitions in Fatima, he at first laughed amusedly, made some sarcastic jokes about it, and declared that such things suited only people with a poor, medieval mentality. But when he heard that four thousand people went to Fatima on July 13, he realized that it was quickly becoming a serious problem.

In fact, central authorities in Lisbon began sending him requests for an explanation. These requests were formulated so that they sounded like reprimands. How could such a thing be justified? How was it possible that he, the person responsible for the local government, was not able to put a stop to such a scandal that made everyone laugh?

De Oliveira was furious. He decided to take care of the problem personally. He began writing sarcastic articles for *O Ouriense,* a newspaper that he published. He spread rumors and ridiculed the apparitions, appealing to science, reason, and common sense. Few people, though, read his newspaper. Those who did paid little attention to what he wrote.

As time went on, he realized that the date for the next apparition, August 13, was fast approaching. His friends informed him that the flow of pilgrims to the site of the apparitions in Fatima was growing day by day, and that a much larger crowd was expected than in the previous month.

Useless Threats

Artur de Oliveira Santos decided to gather together the people responsible for such an act of insubordination. He sent messages to Antonio dos Santos and Manuel Marto, the visionaries' parents, summoning them and their children to a meeting with him. The meeting was set for Saturday, August 11, at noon.

Antonio dos Santos was worried. He feared that he would be punished if he did not go. Early in the morning he and Lucia went to the meeting. Manuel Marto also decided he would obey, but he went alone.

"Why didn't you bring your children as I told you?" the mayor asked grumpily.

"It's far away and the children don't know how to ride," Manuel Marto answered resolutely.

The mayor was furious. He knew that people were afraid of him, and he used this to his advantage. But Marto did not lose his composure. His conscience was peaceful.

Artur de Oliveira began to interrogate Lucia. The child answered timidly in a tense voice.

"What's this about a secret?" de Oliveira asked haughtily.

Lucia looked down and did not answer.

"You have to answer when I speak," the mayor thundered. "Otherwise I'll have your tongue pulled out."

Lucia grew pale and clutched the knee of her father, who was sitting next to her.

The mayor realized that he had gone too far. He turned to Antonio dos Santos and said, "Do you believe what your daughter is saying?"

"It's women's stuff," Antonio answered.

"And you?" he asked Manuel Marto.

"My children and I both feel the same," Jacinta's father answered dryly.

"So you believe them," the mayor sneered.

"Yes, I believe what the children are saying."

Since it was an official interrogation, people were there recording everything the men said. Upon hearing Manuel Marto's response, they all began to laugh, but Manuel remained steadfast and undaunted by the mayor's ire. The officials realized that they were getting nowhere. Once again the mayor threatened Lucia before finally dismissing them.

Artur de Oliveira had failed. August 13 was two days away, and he had not succeeded. The authorities in Lisbon had made their wishes clear. He was supposed to put an end to the whole matter, and he had failed.

The Kidnapping of the Children

He decided, therefore, to use more force. August 13 was a Monday. Early that morning, Artur de Oliveira traveled to Fatima and went straight to the Martos' residence. "I, too, want to be present at the miracle," he said.

Manuel looked at him suspiciously.

"Where are the children?" the mayor asked innocently. "I'll take them to Cova da Iria in my carriage, so that they don't get tired."

"Thank you," Manuel answered. "You don't have to go to the trouble of doing that."

"It would be a pleasure to be of some service, but I don't see them here."

"They are outside tending the sheep."

"But aren't they going to their meeting?"

"They know when they should be back with the sheep in order to get ready to go to Cova da Iria."

At that very moment they heard the bleating of the sheep. Francisco and Jacinta said goodbye to Lucia, who was continuing on. They put the sheep in their pen.

The mayor once again began to press Mr. Marto to let him personally accompany the visionaries to Cova da Iria. "I want to stop in Fatima, so I can question the children in the presence of the pastor of the parish," he said, trying to sound more convincing.

Manuel Marto gave in. The parish priest was someone to whom you should never say no. Perhaps an appointment had been set up. Nonetheless, he decided to accompany them.

"We should also take the other girl," the mayor said.

Manuel took Francisco and Jacinta by the hand and went to the home of Antonio dos Santos. He spoke with him and his wife, Maria

Rosa. He expressed his concerns. He told them that he did not trust the mayor. "We have to stay close to our children," he added.

"I agree," Antonio dos Santos answered.

When Lucia was ready, the men and their children went together to the nearby square, where the mayor's carriage was parked, and got in.

The two men sensed that something might not be right. In reality, the astute politician had prepared a trap. When they arrived in Fatima, he had them get out of the carriage, and together they went in to meet the parish priest. When they came out he had the three children get into the carriage. However, before their parents could get in, he whipped the horse and they went galloping off in the direction of Cova da Iria.

Antonio and Manuel sadly looked at each other and started on foot.

When they got to a fork in the road, the mayor steered the horse toward Vila Nova de Ourem.

"This isn't the road to Cova da Iria," Lucia said.

"Don't worry. We're going first to Ourem to see the pastor, who is waiting for us there. Then we'll all go together to Cova da Iria in an automobile."

There were pilgrims all along the road en route to the place of the apparitions. The pilgrims recognized the children with the mayor and knew that something suspicious was going on. One person shouted out angrily. Another tried to stop the carriage. Finally, the mayor covered up the little children with a blanket so that no one would see them.

When they arrived in Ourem, Artur de Oliveira took the three visionaries to his office and ordered that they be locked in a room.

"You'll get out of there only when you decide to tell me the secret," he threatened.

A Sweet Fragrance

Meanwhile, a huge crowd was gathering at Cova da Iria, larger than any crowd that people in those parts had ever seen. People were arriving from every direction and by every means: foot, bicycle, horse, mule, and ox-driven carts.

Next to the little oak tree, some people were praying the rosary. It was already noon by then, but the children were nowhere to be found. At a certain point, a man arrived from Fatima and said that the children had been taken away by the mayor from Ourem.

Upon hearing this, the crowd of people expressed their disappointment. People protested, and some began to shout out in anger. Other people started to make angry threats, and an ugly riot might have broken out, but a tremendous clap of thunder shook the skies at that very moment, and the crowd calmed down. The clap of thunder was identical to the one that preceded the apparitions.

The crowd grew silent. Some people were frightened and fled from the little oak tree. Many other people fell to their knees.

Some flashes of lightning followed the clap of thunder. Immediately afterwards, a white, misty cloud floated through the blue sky and settled over the oak tree. Everyone was amazed. After a few minutes, the cloud rose into the air and disappeared.

The trees seemed not to have any branches or leaves, just flowers. The ground was a mosaic of beautiful colors. Even the people's clothing reflected the colors of the rainbow.

"My mother was celebrating her birthday that day," Fr. Valinho recalled. "She decided to go to the site of Mary's alleged apparitions. She would not give in, and she still teased Lucia, but she went there nonetheless.

"When she saw all the people, she was quite impressed. But she didn't see Lucia, Francisco, and Jacinta, and she began to worry. She witnessed all the miracles that the people saw at the hour when Mary was supposed to appear, and she was very struck by them.

"Indeed, from that day on, she began to believe everything Lucia was saying. She told me that she had a very strong sense of a strange and unusual atmosphere in that place. The very colors of nature seemed different, as did the colors of the people's clothing.

"But the most impressive thing, she told me, was the fragrance that the little oak tree gave off, and the mysterious light that surrounded it. It seemed as though there were an invisible presence over that little tree. That day my mother realized that a great mystery was taking place there, and that Lucia, who she thought was lying, was telling the truth."

"Let's Go Kill the Mayor"

"Mary came but did not find the children," people said after things returned to normal. They kept repeating these words in a worried voice, as if they were afraid that Mary was angry.

"Let's go free the children!" a man shouted. "Let's go to Ourem and kill the mayor!"

"The parish priest, too," another man said. "He didn't do a thing to defend the children."

Things were heating up. The crowd walked menacingly in the direction of Ourem, shouting so loud that they could be heard even in Aljustrel.

Manuel Marto, who had gone to Cova da Iria sure that he would find the children there, realized that something serious was about to happen that could not be stopped. He was already saddened by what had happened to his children, and he was afraid that the anger of the crowd might make things worse.

"Calm down," he said, "You must not hurt anyone. Whoever deserves punishment will receive it. We shouldn't do anything that we will later regret."

The good man's words were like a balm. Many people realized that he was right and decided to go home. Yet others continued to protest. A little crowd gathered in Fatima and stood threateningly in front of the house of the pastor of the parish.

In Ourem, in the meantime, the three children were locked in a room at the town hall and were crying, especially Jacinta. "I'm not afraid of dying," she said. "But I want to see my mother first."

"Neither your parents nor my parents came to get us," Lucia answered sadly. "They don't care about us!"

Francisco was sitting next to his sister trying to console her. "Don't cry, Jacinta. Let's offer everything to Jesus for sinners."

They spent all afternoon and all night in that room. The next day they were taken to the mayor's office, and the interrogations began. Artur de Oliveira wanted to know the secret, but the three would not budge. He threatened them, made promises to them, and tried to scare them. He even offered them some gold coins.

It was the afternoon, and he had not been able to obtain anything from the three children. He decided to lock them up in jail with the criminals from the area.

"I'll leave you there until the pot of boiling oil is ready, where you'll end up if you don't reveal the secret," he threatened.

The children were convinced that the mayor was serious. They spent many hours in anguish, praying for courage.

The other prisoners, seeing how scared the three little children were, surrounded them and tried to console them. "Tell the blessed secret. What do you care?" they said, unable to understand why the three were ready to die instead of speaking out.

To distract them, they began to sing. One prisoner began to play the accordion. The three children, who loved music, were deeply moved. Jacinta could not resist and began to dance. One of the prisoners wanted to dance with her, but since she was so small, he took her in his arms and danced, holding her in the air. Jacinta danced and cried.

Then the three children decided to pray the rosary. The prisoners knelt down and prayed with them.

In the evening, the mayor returned to his office. He sent a guard to the prison to give a message to the children: "The boiling oil is ready. Speak up now or die."

Jacinta was the first to be called. Trembling, she followed the guard. She was questioned and threatened, but she did not talk.

Then it was Francisco's turn, and then Lucia's turn. No one revealed the secret.

It was the feast of the Assumption. That morning the mayor summoned the three children and said, "I'll take you home now."

"The Madonna has heard our prayers," Lucia said, hugging her two cousins.

"The Madonna! I'm the one who decided not to kill you. But I'll kill you if you don't stop tricking people!"

Around noon Artur de Oliveira's carriage stopped in front of the house of the parish pastor in Fatima. The mayor had the three children get out and turned them over to the priest, who immediately notified their families.

People recognized the carriage and began to surround it. Threats were made, sticks were waved, and faces looked tense. The parish priest stayed inside his house with the children. He was afraid of being assaulted. When Manuel Marto arrived to take the children away, the priest begged him to speak to the people in order to calm them down.

"They're mad at me, too," the priest said. "They say I'm in cahoots with the mayor, but it isn't true."

Marto went out on the stairway with Jacinta in his arms. "Calm down," he said. "Everything has turned out all right. Let's not make any mistakes ourselves."

A Story Worth Forgetting

"That was a big defeat for the enemies of the faith," Fr. Valinho noted. "Kidnapping the children caused quite a sensation. All right-minded people condemned it.

"Even those who didn't believe in the apparitions sided with the little children. Everyone, even his fellow atheists, condemned the mayor's behavior. As it turned out, it helped the apparitions, because the whole matter was reported in the newspapers, thereby arousing people's curiosity."

"Did the mayor realize how serious his actions were?" we asked.

"The whole episode was very serious. The mayor had disgracefully overstepped his power in dealing with the children. I think he himself knew that his plan of action was disgraceful.

"For this reason, as Sr. Lucia has told me, he tried to soften the pain of taking the children away from their families. In the evening he took them to his home and ordered his wife to prepare a nice meal. Thus the children were able to eat well, play with the mayor's children, and sleep in comfortable beds.

"After he took them home, he tried to make peace with Francisco and Jacinta's father. He invited him to the tavern for a glass of wine. Manuel refused, but when he saw people with sticks in their hands, he realized that he might be able to avoid a brawl by staying by him. So he went to have a drink with him, and then let the mayor take him home in his carriage. Manuel was a very good and very wise person."

"And the children?"

"The children were distressed by the whole affair. It was a terrifying event for them, especially Jacinta. During the days that followed, Aunt Olimpia did not send her out to tend the sheep, and kept her near her so she would forget everything that happened."

"I'm curious, Fr. Valinho. That day the Blessed Virgin certainly knew that the mayor had taken the children away and that they couldn't make it to their appointment. But everyone who was at Cova da Iria said that around noon they observed the same signs that generally occurred before the apparitions: the thunder, the lightning, the little cloud, the colors of the rainbow, the bent branches in the oak tree, and so on. Why? Were those signs just a figment of their imagination?"

"Who knows? Maybe they were a figment of their imagination and maybe not. In light of the fact that there were so many signs and that everyone said they 'saw' or 'heard' them, they probably should be treated as objective phenomena.

"Knowing that the children had been taken to Ourem, the Blessed Virgin probably wished to give the people a sign of her presence, as if to repay them for their thoughtfulness. In fact, that day the signs of a divine presence were so intense that many people who were initially skeptical or doubtful, like my mother, for example, began to believe.

"Moreover, the apparitions at Fatima were not a privilege exclusively reserved for the children. Everyone who took part in them had the impression of 'seeing,' 'hearing,' or 'feeling' something to varying degrees. The apparitions at Fatima were a group phenomenon. During the last apparition, which took place in October, more than a hundred thousand people witnessed a powerful and inexplicable miracle."

"The Blessed Virgin didn't appear to the children on August 13, but we know she did appear a few days later."

"That's exactly what happened. Now I'll take you to the place where that apparition occurred. It's a place that is very close to Aljustrel, called Os Valinhos."

14

MEETING AT OS VALINHOS

The street that crosses Aljustrel ends in an esplanade that is used as a parking lot. We parked our car there and proceeded on foot.

"This place was called 'Os Valinhos,'" Fr. Valinho told us, "because of the rolling land that forms little valleys. If you look closely, you'll notice that it still is the same."

We followed him down a small, rocky road that disappeared among some olive trees. The road went to the edge of a hill, where a fence made out of stones stood in its way. Suddenly it turned to the left and then to the right. Before us, beyond a little wall, stood a marble chapel—a simple structure with a statue of the Blessed Virgin inside.

"After the unfortunate incident at Ourem," Sr. Lucia's nephew continued, "the three children hoped to see the Blessed Virgin within a short time. They had been anxiously waiting for August 13 to arrive, but at the last moment they were prevented from going to the long-awaited appointment. They were sure, though, that the Virgin would not make them wait another month before appearing to them.

"Therefore, as soon as they returned home on the fifteenth, they went to Cova da Iria to pray the rosary. They hoped to have a vision, but nothing happened. During the days that followed, they once again started to take the sheep to pasture, to places near their homes. Their parents were worried that they would be kidnapped again, so they did not want them to go too far away."

With Hope in Their Hearts

"Did they have to wait long?" we asked curiously.

"No, only until Sunday, August 19. Teresa, Lucia's sister, and her husband had invited the three visionaries to dinner to try to distract them a little. So Lucia, Francisco, and Jacinta woke up early and took the sheep out to pasture for a couple of hours.

"When it just started to get hot, they went home and dressed up for ten o'clock Mass. They went to Mass with Teresa and her husband, and afterwards went to Cova da Iria, where they prayed the rosary at the site of the apparitions. Deep in their hearts they were still hoping to see our Lady, but again nothing happened that morning."

"They probably appreciated the invitation to have dinner at Teresa's house," we observed.

"Yes. It was something new, and they always liked new things. About four o'clock in the afternoon," Fr. Valinho recounted, "they went home so that they could take the sheep out for a few more hours.

"However, Aunt Olimpia wanted to keep Jacinta with her. She noticed that the child was still disturbed by the series of unfortunate events. Knowing that a mother's love and affection are the best medicine, she decided to spend the afternoon with Jacinta and asked her son, João, to take Jacinta's place with Francisco.

"Lucia decided to bring the sheep here, to Os Valinhos, because there was plenty of grass on which to graze, and it was also close to the house. Every so often, people were looking for her, and if her mother had to send someone to find her, it was only a short distance.

"Leaving the house, which you can see over there, Lucia, Francisco, and João took the same road that we just took to get here on foot. They walked slowly so that the sheep could graze on the grass. Back then, there were a lot of trees. Since the land wasn't so sunny, grass grew abundantly under the trees."

"So the apparition took place right here."

"They had made it to this point at the foot of the hill when Lucia realized that the light from the sun had suddenly set. She looked around and her face became radiant. She realized the phenomenon that typically preceded the apparitions was occurring.

"She pointed it out to Francisco. He, too, realized what was happening. They felt the characteristic breeze and saw the flash of lightning from the east.

" 'The Madonna is coming,' Lucia said with complete certainty. Suddenly she added worriedly, 'But Jacinta isn't here.'

"She turned to João and said, 'Go call Jacinta. Hurry. Tell her the Madonna is coming.'

"João looked at her, but didn't move. Later he told me that when he heard her, he experienced an overwhelming joy. Before that, he had never taken part in the apparitions because he didn't believe his brother, his sister, and Lucia. But that afternoon, when he just happened to be with them and clearly saw the light of the sun suddenly grow dim, he said to himself joyfully, 'Finally, I, too, will have a chance to see.'

"Lucia insisted, 'João, please go get Jacinta.'

"But he still didn't move.

" 'I'll give you two coins if you go,' Lucia begged. 'One now and one when you return with Jacinta.'

"Lucia," Fr. Valinho commented, as he interrupted his account, "was a very practical child, like all the other children back then. She knew that João could not resist making some money. João considered her offer. Later, he told me on several occasions that he immediately thought the whole thing through in a very practical way.

" 'The Madonna will surely wait to appear until Jacinta is here,' he reasoned. 'So I'll go get my sister, and I'll take the two coins as a reward. Since I can run fast, I'll get here before her and I'll be here in time for the apparition.' He took the coin that Lucia showed him and ran home.

" ' Mama, Lucia wants Jacinta to go to Os Valinhos,' he said as he arrived at the house out of breath. Olimpia was standing in the doorway combing the little girl's hair, who was sitting on a chair.

" ' Why?'

" 'Lucia says that the Madonna is coming.'

"Jacinta's heart skipped a beat. She jumped out of her chair.

" 'Come here so I can fix your hair,' her mother said. The little girl was trembling with excitement. Her little heart was beating rapidly. She slipped out of her mother's arms and began to run next to João."

"Make Two Processional Litters"

"Did João leave his sister alone, so that he could get there first?" we asked Fr. Valinho.

"No. The boy was stronger and faster, but he kept pace with his sister. He knew that the Madonna would wait for her. He picked up speed only when he was near the place where Lucia was waiting, so that he could tell his cousin that Jacinta was coming.

"The little girl didn't even have enough time to ask Lucia what was happening, because, as she was arriving, she saw a second flash of lightning, and Mary was already standing there before them. Once again, she chose to appear over a holm oak tree. This one was taller than the one at Cova da Iria, but not much taller. The oak tree was right there, where the candles are burning."

Fr. Valinho paused for a moment. It was almost completely silent. The flames on the candles flickered from the gentle, steady breeze.

Smoke from the candles had blackened a good portion of the wall.

Some people were walking slowly along the path under the olive trees. In front of us, two girls had stopped to pray. Father interrupted his story, probably so that he would not disturb them as they prayed.

After a few minutes, Fr. Valinho resumed his story.

"As usual, Lucia was the one who spoke with Mary.

" 'What do you want of me?' she asked.

" 'I want you to continue coming to Cova da Iria on the thirteenth day of every month,' Our Lady answered, 'and I want you to continue to pray the rosary every day.'

"Referring to everything that had happened during the previous few days, Lucia asked Mary to perform a miracle so that people might finally believe.

" 'Yes,' the Virgin answered. 'On the last month, in October, I'll perform a miracle so that everyone will believe.'

"Lucia then remembered that many people had asked her to present their prayer requests to the Blessed Mother. She especially remembered some people who were sick.

" 'I will heal some of them during the course of this year,' Mary answered.

" 'What do you want us to do with the money that people leave at Cova da Iria?'

" 'I want you to make two processional litters. I want you and Jacinta to carry one of them, along with two other girls dressed in white. Francisco should carry the other one, along with three boys. The money for the processional litters is for the feast of Our Lady of the Rosary. The remaining money is for a chapel that you will build here.'

"The Blessed Virgin became very sad and added, 'Pray, pray very much, and make sacrifices for sinners, for many souls are going to hell since there is nobody to make sacrifices and intercede for them.'

"She raised her eyes toward the sky and disappeared.

"Jacinta was smiling happily. Even Francisco was radiant. João looked at him and was petrified.

"He had seen nothing. He had only noted that Lucia was talking to someone, and he had heard what she was saying. He had seen Francisco and Jacinta looking at a particular spot above the oak tree. He, too, looked closely at that spot, but he could not see anything.

"He told me that he did recall that something was bending the branches of the oak tree. But that's all. He didn't even sense anything special. 'The only thing I saw,' he told me, 'is that I saw nothing.' "

A New Energy and a New Assurance

As usual, the vision left immense joy in the hearts of the three visionaries. João looked around and had thousands of questions that he wanted to ask, but the three children stood there silently, in ecstasy, still immersed in the surrealistic light.

"What were the three visionaries thinking?" we asked Fr. Valinho.

"The apparition completely blotted from their memories the anguish that they had experienced during their time in prison in Ourem, and the sadness they had experienced when they could not make it to their appointment on the thirteenth at Cova da Iria. The Blessed Virgin's words infused their hearts with a new energy and a new assurance. Because of the reference that Mary made to hell and to the miserable fate that awaits so many sinners, they recalled the terrifying vision of July 13 and were strengthened in their desire to help these unfortunate souls through their prayers and sacrifices, just as the Virgin had requested."

"Why did Lucia want to ask Mary how they should use the money from the offerings?"

"Money," Fr. Valinho responded, "always creates problems when it is connected with a religious event. That is exactly what was happening here in Fatima. From the very beginning, people who attended the apparitions began to leave offerings.

"A very old woman, Maria Carreira, who later became known as 'de Capelinha' and who was one of the very first to believe the visionaries, spontaneously started taking care of the place. She cut the grass around the little oak tree, gathered the fallen leaves, and decorated the site with flowers. She also gathered the offerings and put them aside. It was a small amount.

"But on August 13, a large crowd of seven to eight thousand people came to Cova da Iria. These people were indignant that the children had been kidnapped, and they reacted by making numerous generous offerings as a way of showing their sympathy and solidarity and of asking Mary's forgiveness. The sum of money that Maria de Capelinha collected on that day was quite large.

"She could no longer leave it under the oak tree in a bag. Someone had to take care of the money. Mrs. de Capelinha decided to take the money to Mr. Marto, who refused it. She then went to Antonio dos Santos, Lucia's father, and he, too, was indignant and refused it. She took it to the pastor of the parish, who also refused to take it. The money seemed to be cursed.

" 'I'm going to put it back where I found it,' she said, annoyed.

"The parish pastor tried to calm her down. 'Count it and give it to someone who is trustworthy while we wait to see what happens.'

"Although Maria Carreira had heard his suggestion, she still asked Lucia to seek Mary's advice. This is what Lucia did. This explains her question."

The Fragrant Little Branch

"What happened to the oak tree above which Mary appeared?" we asked.

"It was destroyed," Fr. Valinho answered. "That evening, before going home, Jacinta went up to the oak tree and tore off one of the branches upon which Mary had rested her feet. She pressed it affectionately to her heart and returned to Aljustrel.

"As she walked past Lucia's house, my grandmother, Maria Rosa, was outside with my mother, who was already married and had a little girl, and some other people. Jacinta stopped and said, 'Auntie, we saw the Blessed Virgin at Os Valinhos.' "

"What was your grandmother's reaction?"

"She was always skeptical about the whole story and answered, 'Oh, Jacinta, when will you stop telling lies? You, Lucia, and Francisco are incurable liars. You'll end up in hell. Now the Madonna is following you like a little puppy dog and is appearing everywhere you go.'

"'But we did see her,' Jacinta insisted. 'She stood right on this little branch,' and she showed her the little branch that she had torn off the oak tree.

" 'Let me see,' Maria Rosa said.

"Jacinta gave it to her, and my grandmother smelled it. She smelled a strong, sweet fragrance. 'What's that smell?' she asked. It wasn't the fragrance of roses, carnations, or any other flower that she recognized. Curious, she continued to smell it. But she couldn't identify the smell.

" 'Let us smell it too,' my mother said, and she, too, sniffed it. Then she passed it around to the others who were there, and everyone enjoyed its sweet fragrance, but no one could identify what the fragrance was. This prompted a long discussion. Finally my grandmother said to Jacinta, 'Leave that little branch here and we'll see if someone can figure out what kind of fragrance it's giving off.'

"This had a deep effect on my grandmother. By that time, there were many details that no one could explain. She began to think that there was something to their story. Yet she was afraid of being deceived.

" 'If there were at least one other person who saw her besides the three children ...,' she said over and over again, somewhat discouraged. Jacinta went home and left the little branch with my grandmother. But she returned that evening to get it back. She wanted to show it to her father. Uncle Manuel said that he, too, smelled a strong fragrance coming from the little branch."

"And the tree?" we insisted.

"That's right. You had asked me what happened to the tree. Well, about twenty years went by. Francisco and Jacinta were dead, Lucia was a nun, the Church had approved the apparitions, and even my grandmother believed. She had grown old, but she still came from time to time to take a little walk here and pray near the oak tree that had grown into a large tree full of leaves.

"One day the owner of this land decided to chop down all the trees and burn them, so that he could sell them as charcoal. He began cutting down all the trees that were around. When my grandmother heard what was going on, she was upset. She went to the man and offered to buy the tree above which Mary appeared. 'I'm not interested in those stories,' the man answered. 'Just pay me and I'll give it to you.'

"So the tree that was chopped down was taken to my grandmother's house."

The Tree That Ended Up in Pieces

"She carefully kept it under the porch in front of the house," Fr. Valinho continued. "When pilgrims came to see her and talk to her about the apparitions, she would give them a little piece of that tree as a remembrance. I was eight or ten years old at that time, and I perfectly remember her doing this.

"My brother and I were quite adept at cutting off little pieces of the trunk with a large knife. It was hard work because the trunk had become hard as a rock. One day my brother said, 'José, let's finish it off as quickly as we can. Instead of cutting off little pieces like grandmother wants us to, let's cut off big ones. That way we'll get rid of the tree faster and we'll be finished with it.'

"So we began to carve off big pieces to give to the pilgrims, without letting my grandmother see them. Within a short time, we gave the whole tree away. When my grandmother found out, she was really upset, but it was too late by then."

"Does the story of the tree end there?" we asked curiously. Fr. Valinho was a gold mine of information, and we never grew tired of hearing his stories.

"Many years later, when I was already a priest, I met a count in Lisbon. He invited me to his house and showed me a reliquary. There was a piece of that tree in it.

"He explained that my grandmother had given it to him. He, in turn, probably gave many other people pieces of that precious relic. When my grandmother realized that the apparitions were indeed genuine, she became a jealous custodian of everything that had occurred during the many years that she didn't believe."

Fr. Valinho smiled as he remembered his old grandmother.

"She was an extraordinary woman," he murmured.

We looked around and said a prayer. A light breeze was blowing through the leaves of the olive trees and stirred the flames of the candles. We faintly heard some voices. We saw a group of pilgrims walking down the path. Birds flew out of some branches. We, too, began to walk back to the village.

15

THE CROWD IN SEPTEMBER

Every day people were visiting Aljustrel, which had become famous by then.

"Where are the visionaries' houses?" the visitors asked. Then they would wait for hours, hoping to speak with Lucia, Francisco, and Jacinta. As soon as they could, the three children would flee away.

They left early in the morning with the sheep and tried to return only later in the evening. Before approaching their houses, they scouted around to make sure that no one would see them. Although they wanted to listen to such needy people, they knew that they could not do anything for them but pray.

They were very generous with their prayers. Prayer had become their principal activity during the day. The sheep were very docile and did not require much attention. So the little children had plenty of free time.

In the past, they had spent their time playing. Now they had entered a new reality that had totally changed their lives. They no longer experienced a desire to play, sing, and have fun. They only wanted to pray and make sacrifices, clearly aware of the reality that the Blessed Virgin had revealed to them.

Above all, they continually thought about hell. The dramatic vision they had had on July 13 of souls falling into the flames of hell was still vivid in their minds. Mary's repeated injunctions to pray for the conversion of sinners were more vivid than ever in their hearts.

They particularly recalled Mary's words to them at Os Valinhos in August. With great sadness in her eyes, the Blessed Virgin had told them, "Many people will go to hell because there is no one to pray and to make sacrifices on their behalf." The three children had sensed in her words the sorrow of a mother who was losing her children and an anguished plea for help.

Their innocent hearts and their instinctive generosity could not resist such a plea. "What? Are there people who are being lost forever because there is no one to pray for them?" they wondered. "That's absurd. Here we are. We want to pray and make sacrifices incessantly. We want to save all of them. We want to help all of them."

Love Without Limits

"It's moving to see how the three visionaries responded to Mary's invitation with so much enthusiasm," Fr. Valinho said. "The Blessed Virgin had revealed to them a very serious situation. She had given them some important information.

"She had also revealed a great truth, that of the 'Mystical Body.' According to this teaching, all men, through Jesus Christ, form a single body, a family, and a society, in which good and evil are common. Whoever does evil not only hurts himself but others as well; whoever does good helps his brothers and sisters. This is how people, through prayer and the offering of one's sufferings—which are expressions of love and unselfishness—can help their brothers and sisters who are in danger.

"The three children immediately understood the meaning of this great mystical truth, and their response was wonderful. They tried to dedicate all their free time to prayer. They took it upon themselves to continually offer sacrifices to help their brothers and sisters in danger and to save sinners."

"What thoughts and feelings does Sr. Lucia remember from this period?" we asked.

"My aunt is still moved whenever she recalls those days. While all the people around them were clamoring to know if the apparitions were authentic or not and were continually questioning them to find out the famous secret, the three of them lived their lives immersed in heroic unselfishness. It was the month of August. It was very hot. At certain times of the day, the air was suffocating. Yet the three of them subjected themselves to tormenting sacrifices.

"Sr. Lucia recalls that it was precisely during that month of stifling heat that they forced themselves not to drink any water and to offer this as a sacrifice to the Blessed Mother. They abstained from water up to nine days in a row. They discovered that certain herbs were very bitter and they ate them as a means of mortification.

"Jacinta was once picking some wild fruit and severely scratched her tender skin with some thorns. 'I've found another way of making a sacrifice,' she said enthusiastically. 'You can put your hands in thorns.' "

"Their love and generosity had no limits," we commented with amazement.

"That's true, but maybe they exaggerated. They probably needed a spiritual director who would limit and regulate their altruistic impulses. But you can't order the heart to do something.

"One day while they were going out to pasture, Lucia found a piece of rope, one of those thick, rough ropes that you use for tying down a load on a cart. She picked it up, wondering how she could use it. Playfully, she tied it around her wrist and immediately noticed that the rough and prickly rope hurt her.

" 'Look,' she said to her cousins. 'This rope hurts! We can wear it around our waists and offer the pain to God.'

"Francisco and Jacinta agreed. Lucia cut the rope into three pieces, using the sharp corner of one stone pitted against another as a knife. They each started to wear a piece as a penance, tied around their waists on their bare skin. Either because of the roughness of the rope or because they tied it too tight, it hurt terribly. Jacinta often cried because of the pain but didn't take it off."

"The Whole World Will Be Laughing"

After the apparitions, Cova da Iria was no longer as green and secluded as it had been. It had become a mud bowl. On July 13 and August 13, crowds invaded it and destroyed everything.

The fields that had been cultivated no longer existed. The land, which belonged to Lucia's family, had consisted of rich soil that bore abundant fruit. Every year the family obtained potatoes, corn, beans, olives, and nuts from that land.

A part of these gifts from God was used for their own nourishment, while the other part was sold. But within two months, the dos Santos family had completely lost the harvest from Cova da Iria. The fertile land, trampled by thousands of people and crisscrossed by horses, mules, carts, and automobiles, was now lost.

The damage was extensive. Antonio, her father, Maria Rosa, her mother, and even Lucia's older sisters felt a sharp stab of pain in their hearts when they saw their property in ruin. It appeared as though a mighty storm and a devastating flood had ravaged it. Furthermore, there was no hint that the catastrophe would ever end. On the contrary, they knew that an even more devastating wave of people was on its way.

"Now that there's nothing to eat, go ask the Lady for something," Maria Rosa said to her daughter, Lucia.

"We should make you eat only what's growing at Cova da Iria," her sisters echoed.

"Who's going to repay me for the serious damage that they did there?" her father, Antonio, asked worriedly.

Lucia experienced no relief from her family's hostility. They continued to think she was a liar, and she suffered because of it.

Locally, the people's attitude continued to be one of condemnation. Very few people believed in the apparitions. Most thought that Lucia had made up the whole story and had her little cousins under her spell. She was the one who was responsible; she was the bad one; she was the obstinate one. She had to be careful when she was out walking alone. Women had threatened her. Some had even assaulted her.

As news of the apparitions spread throughout Portugal, anger and skepticism grew among the local people. Seeing so many people arrive from afar, they feared even more that they were the victims of some kind of fraud. "If everything turns out to be false, the whole world will be laughing at us," they said.

More and more, they felt certain that no such thing could happen in their forsaken and forgotten land. "Did the Madonna have to come *here?*" they asked sarcastically. "Did she have to appear to these three ignorant and illiterate children? Come on, let's not joke around."

Church authorities were afraid of being involved in a colossal fraud, so they kept their distance. They did not participate in the apparitions, nor did they make any judgments, nor did they want to be seen with the visionaries.

The three children were completely isolated. People avoided them like the plague. The only people who sought them out were strangers, but the children were afraid of them and tried to avoid them.

"Invented by the Priests"

Even if the people of Fatima did not believe in the apparitions, they did not appreciate it when strangers came and ridiculed the apparitions and made fun of the visionaries. Thus, they refused to take part in the campaign that the anticlerics were waging throughout the country against the apparitions in Fatima.

The ruling class in Portugal at that time was comprised of anticlerics and Masons. They were conducting a violent campaign against religion throughout the country. Everything that was happening at Fatima irritated both the central and regional governments. For them, the eight thousand people who traveled to Cova da Iria on August 13 for the apparitions were a nightmare. For this reason, orders were given from on high to put an end to the whole affair—at any cost.

September 13 was drawing near. The hearts of the three visionaries were filled with joy as they thought about this day, since they would experience once again an indescribable encounter from on high. At the same time, though, the growing tension and oppression that they felt in the air all around them frightened them.

Newspapers were publishing articles. Politicians were arguing. People were talking about the apparitions in Lisbon, in Porto, and in all the cities, both big and small, throughout the country. Those in authority were growing increasingly anxious by all this talk. They wanted to put an end to all this embarrassment.

Most newspaper articles consisted of reports that twisted the facts, ridiculed the visionaries, and invented absurd stories. Their aim, which they pursued with a diabolical pleasure, was only to discredit what they called "the new miracle factory that was invented by the priests." The more tolerant reports classified the phenomenon as group hypnosis.

In any case, insults against religion were pouring forth. In the end, though, these disdainful articles had the opposite effect. Because of these articles, which were published in newspapers with a nationwide circulation, news about the apparitions resounded throughout the country. When people read about what was happening, they did not pay the least attention to the commentaries. They rushed to Fatima to see for themselves.

By the end of August, the countryside was filled with handbills that contained raging invectives against the purported apparitions and against priests. They invited people to a public meeting that would be held in the town square on the following Sunday morning, after the ten o'clock Mass in the parish. The purpose of the meeting was to expose the fraud of Cova da Iria.

The Braying of Donkeys

A man named José do Vale, the editor of a newspaper called *O Mundo*, was at the origins of this initiative. He was an anarchist and an atheist, and some friends who shared his political and religious convictions supported him.

News about the meeting spread throughout the countryside, and everyone was talking about it. The pastor of the parish in Fatima was afraid that disorder would break out and canceled ten o'clock Mass for that Sunday, which was the principal Mass. The visionaries' parents and relatives were angry, but they knew they could not do anything. Any type of reaction would be dangerous.

Once again, they vented their anger on the children. "Please confess that you made everything up so that we can finally live in peace," they begged. They knew that the children were in great danger at that point, and they decided to send them out of the area.

But José do Vale's initiative ended in failure. The people of Aljustrel and Fatima did not believe in the apparitions, but they respected God and religion. They did not want to have anything to do with an avowed atheist, anticleric, and Mason. When José do Vale and his friends arrived at the town square for the meeting, no one was there.

They were indignant. They felt defeated, and they also felt that the people were laughing at them. They decided to go to Cova da Iria. Thinking that people would be gathered there to pray, they decided to hold their meeting there.

When they arrived at the clearing, they looked around in amazement. There was no one at Cova da Iria—not a single soul. Near the site of the apparitions, some thirty or more donkeys were tied together in the shade of some trees.

"What are all these asses doing here?" José do Vale asked his friends. The answer was quick to come. No sooner had he finished speaking, the donkeys began to bray frantically. The noise was deafening.

Amid the braying, José do Vale also heard the sound of laughter. He realized at that point that he had fallen in a trap that the people of Fatima had planted. Anticipating that the fanatic would go to Cova da Iria when he saw that there was no one in the town square, they decided to welcome him in a way that befitted him so he would know what they thought about his ideas.

They had tied the donkeys to the trees so that they would be the ones to attend his meeting. As José do Vale approached the site, some young boys, who were hiding among the donkeys, opened up some bottles filled with a liquid that smelled disgusting. They held them to the noses of the donkeys, thereby inciting their frantic brays.

A Sad Denial

Fanatical anticlerics were not the only people who visited the area. Important people, who did not have the least fear of letting people know that they believed the children, also visited. The clergy, however, remained aloof.

The Church is always very prudent in such matters. For this reason, the pastor of the parish in Fatima never wished to divulge his own feelings in the matter. However, when the mayor of Ourem tried to implicate him in the incident involving the "kidnapping" of the three children, he sent a long, open letter to the newspaper in Vila Nova de Ourem, *O Ouriense*, and the newspaper in Lisbon, *A Ordem*, in which he denied any involvement.

"With disgust in my heart as a Catholic priest, I wish to make plain and assure all those who have knowledge or who have come to know of the rumor that I was an accomplice in the abduction of the little children who said they saw the Virgin Mary in this parish, that I consider it so unjust as well as insidious a calumny, declaring to everyone that I did not take part, in the smallest way, whether directly or indirectly, in so odious and sacrilegious an act."

After having explained how the events developed, he added, "If believers are speaking out about my absence at the site as pastor of the parish, no less would unbelievers be speaking out about my presence there, to the detriment of the truth of the facts. The Virgin Mother of God does not need the presence of a parish priest to show her goodness.

"It is necessary that the enemies of religion do not tarnish the luster of her benevolence by attributing the people's belief to the presence or counsel of the parish pastor, because faith is a gift from God and not from a priest. This is the real reason for my absence and apparent indifference in so sublime and marvelous a matter. This is why I have never manifested my own opinion, in spite of the thousands of questions and letters directed to me."

This statement reveals to us that the pastor of the parish in Fatima had actually formed a serious opinion on the matter. Yet he was careful not to express it, and rightly so.

There were a number of people who openly endorsed the apparitions, such as some rich ladies who came from Lisbon to attend the apparitions.

One person who demonstrated great respect for the children from the very beginning was Dr. Carlos de Azeveda Mendes di Torres Novas. In her memoirs, Lucia fondly remembers her first meeting with this gentleman, who was young and unmarried at the time. At the beginning of September of 1917, as the day of the fifth apparition was approaching, Dr. Mendes decided to seek out the young visionary. Lucia's subsequent account of the meeting is extraordinary, because it reveals both the little girl's witty character and her extraordinary insight. For this reason, we wish to relate this meeting in the visionary's own words.

A Good Giant

"It was during that month," Sr. Lucia wrote, "that a young man appeared, who made me tremble from fear because of his tall stature. When he entered the house looking for me, he was so tall he had to stoop down to get through the door. I thought I was in the presence of a German.

"Since we were at war and families had the habit of threatening their children by saying, 'There's a German coming to kill you,' I thought the end was near. My terror did not escape the young man's gaze, and he tried to calm me down by having me sit on his lap while he gently asked me questions. When he finished with his questions, he asked my mother if she would let me show him the site of the apparitions and pray there together.

"She gave her permission and we were off. I was trembling from fear because I was alone on the path with a stranger. Yet I was reassured by the thought that I would see the Lord and the Madonna if I were killed.

"When we arrived at the site, he knelt down and asked me to pray the rosary with him and ask Mary for a blessing that he desired very much: that a certain girl would consent to receive the sacrament of matrimony with him. I found his request rather strange and thought, 'If she's as afraid as I am, she'll never say yes!'

"When we finished the rosary, the kind man accompanied me back to my village and graciously bade farewell, asking me to pray for his request. Then I ran as fast as I could to my aunt and uncle's house, fearing that he would come back.

"You can imagine my surprise when suddenly, on October 13, after the apparition, I found myself in that young man's arms as he carried me above the people's heads. They really wanted him to do it so that everyone could see me. After a short distance, the kind man, who couldn't see where he was going, tripped on some stones and fell down. I didn't fall down because the crowd held me up.

"He disappeared but reappeared some time later with the girl, who had become his wife. He came to thank the Holy Virgin for the grace he had received and to ask her for a special blessing. Today that young man is Dr. Carlos Mendes di Torres Novas."

Suffering Humanity

On the evening of September 12, pilgrims, most of whom were strangers to the area, started flowing into Fatima, Aljustrel, and Cova da Iria. People were camping out everywhere. Fortunately, the weather was good. There was no inconvenience to sleeping outdoors.

People besieged the homes of Francisco, Jacinta, and Lucia, and their owners did not know how to defend their homes. Maria Rosa, Olimpia, and their husbands and their children were friendly people with good hearts. They did not have the courage to chase away the intruders, who, for the most part, were troubled by painful problems.

On the morning of the thirteenth, the number of pilgrims increased considerably. Carts and groups of people on foot were arriving constantly, as well as automobiles from afar. The roads around Aljustrel were swarming with people.

Most of them were believers. Very few were simply curious. As the people walked to Cova da Iria, they prayed and sang sacred hymns.

Lucia, Francisco, and Jacinta remained locked in their homes until eleven o'clock in the morning. Then they got ready for their appointment with the Virgin Mary.

Lucia went to her cousins' house. She met them there and they left together, accompanied by some relatives.

A crowd in the street that was waiting for them surrounded them. The crowd began to follow them, growing in number as they walked along.

Everything that was happening was unprecedented. The three children were pale and frightened. There were constant interruptions en route. People fell to their knees in the middle of the road and shouted out their problems.

"For the love of God, ask the Madonna to heal my crippled son."

"My son is blind, have pity and pray for him."

"My son is deaf. Ask for the grace that he might hear."

"Ask the Blessed Virgin to bring my husband back from the war."

"I'm a sinner. Tell the Virgin Mary to look down upon me."

Their voices resounded through the air, and their faces were covered with tears. The children were moved as they saw them and listened to them. Jacinta, Lucia, and Francisco walked up to the people who were kneeling before them and tried to help them get up.

"We will pray for you ... we will remember you ... but please get up," the children responded. They were struck by all the suffering.

This scene made a deep impression on Lucia. Remembering it as an adult, she wrote in her memoirs, "When I read those delightful passages in the New Testament about Jesus as he wandered through Palestine, I remember everything that happened in Aljustrel when I was a child. Jesus let me contemplate those same scenes on the road and the poor pathways that lead from Aljustrel to Cova da Iria.

"I thanked him by offering him the faith of those good Portuguese people. If those people prostrated themselves before three miserable children simply because they were mercifully granted the grace to speak with the Mother of God, imagine what they would do if they saw Jesus himself standing before them."

How Many Blessed Virgins Are There in Heaven?

That day the trip was long and tiring. Newspapers reported that between twenty-five and thirty thousand people were present at Cova da Iria on September 13—an inconceivable size crowd for the people of Fatima. The path to the site of the apparitions was jammed. It was difficult to walk. Seminarians and priests were also present in the crowd.

Lucia, Francisco, and Jacinta arrived at Cova de Iria at around noon. When they arrived at the little holm oak where the apparitions took place, they knelt down to pray the rosary and the people did likewise. Intense devotion pervaded the atmosphere. At a certain point, Lucia interrupted her prayer, rose to her feet, turned to the crowd, and said, "The Blessed Virgin is coming."

Everyone saw a flash of lightning as the intensity of the sun diminished. They felt a strange breeze. There was much tension in the air. Then Lucia fell to her knees. Mary was there before her.

"What do you want of me?" Lucia asked.

"That you continue to pray the rosary every day so that the war will end."

Referring to what she had already told them in their previous encounters, Mary added, "Do not miss October 13. On that day you will also see the Lord, Our Lady of Sorrows, Our Lady of Mount Carmel, and St. Joseph with the Child Jesus to bless the world. God is pleased with your sacrifices, but he does not want you to sleep with the rope. Only wear it during the day."

"People have begged me to ask you many things," Lucia said. "The healing of some sick people, of a deaf-mute ..."

"Yes, I will heal a few of them, but not others. In October I will perform a miracle so that everyone might believe."

Lucia rose to her feet and cried out to the crowd, "If you want to see her, look over there."

At that moment the Virgin began to rise up in the blue sky. Everybody gazed to the east, and many people said that they saw a ball of light moving rapidly in that direction.

The Blessed Virgin did not say anything new in this encounter, according to Lucia's account at the time. She did, however, speak about her coming appearance in October, when she promised that a mighty miracle would take place and that other heavenly beings would be there, including Jesus and St. Joseph. She also said that the Child Jesus would be there, as well as Our Lady of Sorrow and Our Lady of Mount Carmel. What did this mean?

We posed this question to Fr. Valinho.

"Father, when Jesus died, he was an adult. Why did Mary tell the visionaries that they would see a vision of the Child Jesus? Also, why did she say that on October 13 they would also see Our Lady of Sorrows and Our Lady of Mount Carmel? How many Blessed Virgins are there in heaven?"

Fr. Valinho listened to our rather naive questions and smiled with amusement. He knew they were simply the result of superficial and foolish curiosity, but he answered nonetheless.

"There is only one Jesus in heaven, the one who lived in the Holy Land two thousand years ago and who rose to the glory of the Father with his body after his resurrection from the dead. There is only one Mary, the mother of Jesus, who is also in heaven in body and soul.

"An apparition is a mystical phenomenon, a special experience that mysteriously recalls particular events. It symbolizes a situation, a truth, or a historical event that took place or that will take place. The dimensions in which these apparitions occur are outside our categories of space and time.

"The image of the Child Jesus is there to remind us of an event that already took place, the mystery of the incarnation of Christ, of God who became a child, who was born of Mary. Our Lady of Sorrows and Our Lady of Mount Carmel are one and the same person—Mary of Nazareth, the mother of Jesus, who is venerated by the faithful under the various names that represent the different facets of her spiritual personality. But it's clear that it's always the same person. In heaven there is only one Jesus and one Blessed Virgin, his mother."

16

THE DANCE OF THE SUN

The big day was drawing near. For six months the Virgin Mary had been telling the three visionaries that a miracle would take place on October 13 so everyone would believe. The visionaries had told the people about it. The news had spread. It was widely reported in the newspapers, and people's expectations were growing.

Everyone was involved. Those who believed in the apparitions—mostly consisting of poor people who were highly sensitive to religious matters—awaited the day when they would be able to "rejoice" in the presence of the supernatural and experience God's consolation. Skeptics were sure that the publicized miracle would never happen, and that their theories of fraud and mass hypnosis would triumph in the end.

Finally, the enemies of religion, consisting of atheists, anticlerics, and Masons, who were also skeptics, were certain that the miracle would not happen. They hoped to take advantage of the occasion to attack the Church once again.

The wait was agonizing, more than we can imagine in looking back after so many years. All the different categories of people mentioned above felt obliged to make the appointment at Cova da Iria. They all wished to be present in order to see their expectations come true. If twenty-five to thirty thousand people were at Cova da Iria in September, more than double that number were expected on October 13.

"You're the Devil's Children"

As the date drew near, troubles and fears multiplied. There were all kinds of rumors. There was even some talk of assaults and bomb attacks. People were saying that anarchists were ready to use the enormous gathering of people in order to make a bloody demonstration against the government and against religion.

The people of Fatima and Aljustrel were frightened. They blamed the visionaries.

"We're all going to die because of you," they said.

"You don't have any conscience. You're the devil's children."

"It would have been better if we had cut your heads off."

They also blamed the visionaries' families.

"The parents of those frauds are the ones who are most at fault, because they didn't punish them."

"If they were my children, they would have already retracted everything."

"I would have sent them to jail if they were my children."

The three children's brothers and sisters were embarrassed to leave the house. Everyone was pointing fingers at their parents.

Manuel Marto and his wife, Olimpia, endured the hostility in silence, because they believed Francisco and Jacinta. Antonio and Maria dos Santos, on the other hand, did not believe Lucia. They were angry with her and constantly encouraged her to recant.

"You must say that you made everything up," they told her repeatedly.

"I can't take back what I said because I did see her," Lucia responded in tears. But neither one believed her.

"You're as stubborn as a mule. You don't care at all about your family," her mother retorted.

Even Lucia's sisters did not give their poor sister any respite. "Please take back everything, else we'll die."

"They'll throw bombs and our house will be destroyed."

Some priests from the area were asked to try to convince the three children that they should confess that everything was a lie. The tension of the constant interrogations left Lucia, Francisco, and Jacinta in tears, but they did not allow themselves to be intimidated. "We saw her," they said over and over. "We can't say anything that's different from that, or else it would be a lie."

One of Lucia's aunts, who lived a distance from Fatima, feared for their safety and came to Aljustrel. "I heard they want to kill my niece," she said, "so I came to get her. I'll take her to my house. We live in another district, and no one there can hurt her."

The constant stress that the three children were under was enough to break anyone. Yet they seemed to have nerves of steel. Everything that was happening worried them, especially the sorrow and the fear that they saw on the faces of their family members. But peacefully they said over and over, "The Madonna told us that nothing bad would happen."

On the morning of October 12, Maria Rosa woke Lucia up at the break of dawn.

"It's best that we go to confession," she said with anguish in her voice. "Tomorrow Mary won't perform a miracle and the people will kill us. It's best that we be in God's graces."

Smiling, Lucia answered: "If you want to go to confession, Mama, I'm prepared to go with you to the church. But you shouldn't do it because you're afraid they're going to kill us. I'm sure that tomorrow our Lady will perform a miracle and that nothing bad will happen to us."

The People on the Way

That year October 13 fell on a Saturday. Early in the morning, people literally began to invade Fatima. By noon, it was impossible to walk through the streets.

The weather was terrible. It was raining over the entire plateau of the Estremadura. It was a light rain but constant enough to penetrate the earth and to penetrate people to the bone. But it did not stop the constant flow of people.

For several weeks, newspapers had been publishing articles about the miracle that was supposed to occur. Skepticism and sarcasm characterized the articles. As a result, the entire country knew about the event. People were coming *en masse* to Fatima from distant regions.

The principal newspapers sent their reporters. "Nothing's going to happen," their editors said, "but you have to be there. You never know."

Thanks to these journalists, it is still possible for us to know everything that happened that day, even after so many years have gone by. Reading their articles, it is surprising to see that extraordinary tension and emotion pervade their reports. There are no exceptions. Even correspondents from the anticlerical newspapers filed reports that still make a person shiver when they are read today.

First of all, they gave an eyewitness account of the flow of people.

"The cities, towns, and villages of the countryside were depopulated," the correspondent of *O Dia* wrote. "Beginning the night before, groups of pilgrims were heading toward Fatima. The fishermen of Vieira abandoned their black, wooden houses and left their poor nets on the bank of the sea.

"Across the hills and through the pine forests they arrived on foot, with their wool socks pulled up over their muscular legs, their flowing cloaks over their shoulders, and a bag of supplies on their heads....

Workmen from Marimba, laborers from Monte Real, Cortes, Marrazes, inhabitants from the distant mountains of Soubio, Minde, and Louriçal, people from every place that word of the miracle had reached left their houses and their fields to come to Fatima."

How many people were there? The month before, the crowd at Cova da Iria had reached an incredible twenty-five to thirty thousand people. According to the newspapers, about eighty to a hundred thousand people were there for this meeting, and some even mentioned a hundred and thirty thousand people.

People tried to camp out as best they could during the night. The field was now one immense mud puddle, and the mule paths were impassable.

It never stopped raining. By morning people were soaking wet. They felt as though their clothes were made of lead. The horrible weather continued. Yet people continued to arrive.

The crowd that surrounded Cova da Iria was divided into two groups. Those who believed waited patiently in the rain without moving. Their feet were planted in the mud as they prayed and sang.

Those who were skeptical or simply curious were impatient. They perched themselves under trees or next to rocks to protect themselves from the rain. Some locked themselves up in their cars. They all were cursing the weather and the visionaries and sneering at those people who were praying.

In the Rain

People surrounded the homes of Lucia and Francisco and Jacinta. Many had entered their houses and filled the various rooms. "We couldn't send them away," Manuel Marto, who was very good-hearted, later explained. "It was raining outside, and they wanted some shelter."

At Lucia's house, the atmosphere was different from usual. For the first time, Maria Rosa seemed to be deeply concerned about her daughter's fate. She noticed that the young girl had tears in her eyes as she was getting dressed.

"Don't be afraid, Mama," Lucia told her when she noticed her mother's anguish. "You can be sure that nothing will happen to me."

Her words did not have a calming effect on Maria Rosa. She was feeling guilty for having scolded the child so often. "If my daughter has to die," she said resolutely at one point, "I want to be with her."

She called her husband. "Antonio, let us go with Lucia to Cova da Iria," she said.

They left the house around eleven o'clock and went to the home of the Marto family. It took a lot of effort to make their way in.

Manuel and Olimpia, Francisco and Jacinta's parents, were delighted to see them. "You give us courage," Manuel said. "With you at our side, we'll feel safer."

"Why?" Antonio asked.

"Friends have said that we are in greater danger than our children," Manuel answered. "People will probably respect such little creatures, but they could get angry with us. Olimpia, my wife, is frightened. She's constantly praying to the Blessed Mother. I'm not afraid. I'm sure that our children have always told the truth."

Along the way, scenes from the month before were repeated. As the children walked by, people knelt on the ground and asked for prayer. The road was all muddy, but even women with jewels and expensive dresses were falling to their knees and crying.

Jacinta was worried about her father. She kept looking back and saying with her soft voice, "Don't crush my father."

Cova da Iria was a human jungle. People were everywhere. Many tried to protect themselves with umbrellas, but most of the people were standing in the rain without any protection. Women had their soaking wet shawls over their heads .

"Let the children who see Mary pass through," said the men who "escorted" the visionaries. People stood aside and were deeply moved as they watched the children go by.

Lucia, Francisco, and Jacinta, along with their parents, took their place next to the little holm oak. In reality, though, there was little left of the small tree. It had been reduced to a stump, without any leaves or branches. People had decorated it with silk bows and wild flowers in order to hide its miserable condition.

Lucia knelt down to pray the rosary. Immediately she rose and turned to the people around her. "Close your umbrellas, and let's pray the rosary," she said.

"The girl said to close the umbrellas," the people echoed to those around. Within minutes, all the umbrellas were closed. Everyone was quiet. People stood motionless under the pouring rain, responding in chorus as Lucia led them in each Hail Mary of the rosary.

The prayer time was short. Lucia saw a flash of lightning, and the Blessed Virgin was already standing above the remains of the little holm oak.

"What do you want of me?" the little girl asked.

"I want a chapel to be built here in my honor," Mary answered. Then she added, "I am Our Lady of the Rosary. Continue to pray the rosary every day. The war will end and the soldiers will soon return to their homes."

"I have a lot of things to ask you. If you will heal some of the sick people and convert some sinners ...," Lucia said.

"Some yes and some no," Our Lady answered. "They must mend their ways and ask forgiveness for their sins, in order not to offend our Lord, who is already too much offended."

The Miracle

Then the Blessed Virgin began to rise up into the sky. Lucia later recounted that as she rose, "she opened her hands, and an enormous ray of light came out from her hands and parted the clouds in order to make the sun appear. That ray of light was reflected by the sun and fell to the earth, enveloping the Virgin as she rose slowly into the sky.

"When the Madonna was near the sun, St. Joseph appeared at her side with the Child Jesus. He seemed to be blessing the world, tracing the sign of the cross with his hand. After a while, when that apparition had disappeared, I saw Our Lord and Our Lady, who appeared to be Our Lady of Sorrows. Our Lord seemed to be blessing the world, just as St. Joseph had. His vision disappeared, and I seemed to see the Madonna again, who looked like Our Lady of Mount Carmel."

Lucia was ecstatic, turned to the people, and shouted, "Look at the sun."

The sun had broken through the clouds and was shining in the blue sky. But it looked unusual. It was whirling around on its own axis. Its light was intense, but the people could look at it with the naked eye, without being blinded. It was spinning off rays of different colors, which fell to the ground and surrealistically transformed the landscape. Its light turned blue, a fantastic blue. Then it suddenly turned intensely yellow before turning blue once again.

The crowd was fascinated by what they saw. All the people fell to their knees, crying out in astonishment.

"A miracle!"

"What a wonder!"

"Praise God!"

Their cries spread through Cova da Iria like an immense prayer.

Suddenly the sun began to dance. It leapt. Then it stopped but began to jump and dance. It left the sky and raced towards the earth. Then it drew back to its place in the sky. It descended again in a terrifying flight, then ascended.

Now the people were terrified.

"Help us, O Mary!"

"We're all going to die!"

"Forgive us our sins!"

"Save us, Lord!"

Their terror lasted for several minutes that seemed like they would never end. Then the sun ascended to its place in the sky and whirled around, creating a light show that had never been seen before. It was a fantastic phenomenon, and everyone who was there witnessed it.

Besides this magnificent spectacle of the sun, there was another extraordinary and inexplicable phenomenon. The people, who had been under the pouring rain for hours and hours, had been soaking wet. Suddenly, though, their clothing was perfectly dry, totally dry, as though it had never rained. They looked at each other in amazement, felt their clothing, looked at the sky, then fell to their knees in the mud and wept with emotion.

"Most Holy Mother, Patroness of Portugal, have pity on us, poor sinners!"

"It Was Not Mass Hallucination"

The people were deeply impressed by all this. This is clear from the newspaper reports that followed. All of them, including the anticlerical newspapers that had sent their reporters with orders to ridicule it as a comedy, published ample reports objectively telling everything that happened, and making it clear that it was a grandiose phenomenon for which there was absolutely no explanation.

Avelino de Almeida, the special correspondent for the anticlerical newspaper *O Secolo*, wrote: "The sun looked like a disk of dull silver, and it was possible to look straight at it without the least effort. To the astonished eyes of that people, whose attitude transports us back to biblical times, and who, ashen with terror, with heads uncovered, gazed into the blue sky, the sun tremble, the sun made brusque movements, never seen before, that defied all cosmic laws. The sun danced, according to the typical expression of the peasants."

The correspondent of *O Dia* added, "Everyone was crying, with their rosaries in their hands, because of the magnificent impression that the long-awaited miracle caused. The few minutes seemed like hours because they were so impressed."

During the following days, the newspapers amply documented the fact that the phenomenon was not only observed at Cova da Iria. It was also observed in other places, some even several hundred miles from Fatima.

"This is extremely important," Fr. Valinho said in response to our request for his interpretation. "It shows that the crowd present at the apparition wasn't suffering from mass hallucination. Mary knew that skeptics would immediately say that everything that happened was the result of hallucination. That's why the Blessed Virgin made sure that the phenomenon was observed around Portugal.

"In the days following the event, newspapers published many eyewitness reports. Letters arrived by mail. Some were important people, such as the poet Alfonso Lopez Vieira, who saw the phenomenon from his house at San Pietro di Moel, which is twenty-five miles from Fatima.

"Fr. Ignazio Lourenço, who saw it from Alburitel, also wrote an account. Fr. Lourenço recalls that several dozen people from his town also saw it.

" 'People ran into the streets crying and pointing to the sun,' he wrote in his eyewitness report. 'It was not mass hallucination and it was not a natural phenomenon because no astronomical observatory recorded any kind of abnormality. The event, which people of every age, culture, social class, and religious faith in Cova da Iria and other places in Portugal observed and saw, has no explanation, and will therefore be remembered as a marvelous miracle.' "

17

NO PEACE

The Blessed Virgin did all that she had promised in May when she had appeared to Lucia, Francisco, and Jacinta. She returned on six different occasions, on the thirteenth of every month. During her last visit, she performed the great miracle that she had previously announced.

Mary had given the three visionaries messages, prophecies, and a secret, and had entrusted to them the task of continuing that extraordinary event as the years went on.

After the apparition in October, life in Fatima returned to normal. Little by little, the number of people who visited Cova da Iria out of curiosity or to pray dwindled. The three visionaries themselves were no longer the center of attention.

During the second apparition in June, Mary had told the three children that they should learn to read. Therefore, Lucia, Jacinta, and Francisco started to go to school. Because of the confusion caused by the constant flow of visitors, Lucia's parents were forced to sell most of their sheep, keeping only three. The three sheep no longer required very much work, and Lucia was able to attend school. Since Francisco and Jacinta never wanted to be apart from their cousin, they left the care of their sheep to their brother, João, and began to go to school also.

Lucia loved to study and devoted herself to her studies with zeal. Francisco and Jacinta, on the other hand, were indifferent and little motivated. "We must die," they told their little cousin. "The Madonna promised us that she would soon take us to heaven. Why should we study? It's better that we devote the time to prayer."

"There's No Reason for Knowing How to Read"

"The three children felt that the time had come to resume normal life once again," Fr. Valinho explained. "It meant, though, that their life would be just like the lives of other children their age. But this was impossible. They were definitely different from others.

"They could not ignore everything that had happened to them. People knew. Their friends at school knew. The three children themselves had undergone some incredible experiences that had strongly changed their thoughts, aspirations, and ways of seeing the world and life. For this reason, even school was now complicated for them."

"Are there any testimonies of this situation?" we asked.

"One of Francisco's friends from school has left an invaluable testimony that helps us understand how things really were. It was written by Antonio dos Reis, who later became a priest and rector of the seminary in Leiria. He says that their teacher was an unbeliever who teased Francisco and took advantage of every opportunity to ridicule the apparitions.

"This encouraged the other students to do likewise. Everybody laughed at the poor boy, who was withdrawn, quiet, and sad. During recess, the bullies would pull him aside, shove him, and often hit him.

"Francisco put up with it, but he suffered greatly. It's understandable why he was always alone and wasn't enthusiastic about studying. School had become a nightmare for him, and he often played hooky.

"He used to leave with Jacinta and Lucia in the morning, but when they arrived at the church, where they always stopped to pray for a while, he often told them, 'I'll stay here. There's no use in going to school. I must die soon, so there's no reason for knowing how to read. I'll stay here to keep the "Hidden Jesus" company. This way I'll avoid upsetting my teacher and my classmates.' "

Vandals at Work

The anticlerics seemed to be most attentive to what was happening in Fatima during those months. Apparently they felt that the events that were happening there might constitute a serious danger to their ideas and projects. Therefore they were busy at work, while believers, followers, and churchmen were busy discussing and questioning.

The Masonic circles in Lisbon issued their order: "You need to destroy everything at Fatima." Their henchmen began their work.

On the night of October 23-24, barely ten days after the last apparition and the miracle of the sun, some members of a Masonic group from Santarem, the capital of the district in which Fatima was located, together with some friends from Vila Nova de Ourem, organized a punitive raid on Cova da Iria. Using an ax, they cut down the little holm oak where Mary appeared and carried it off, along with the other objects that were at the site. These included a little table that served as an altar, a framed photo of the Blessed Virgin, two metal lanterns that were hanging over the holm oak, a metal cross, a wooden cross, and some other small devotional items.

The vandals took these things to Santarem. There they organized an exhibition on the square in front of the seminary. People were invited to purchase a ticket to view them. The proceeds of the ticket sales would be used to maintain some school cafeterias. They wanted people to direct their interest to the social needs of the people, not to petty old religious superstitions.

After the theft and the brazen exhibition that followed, these same fanatics organized a sacrilegious procession of the stolen items through the streets of the city. Participants in this "ceremony" sang blasphemous versions of litanies to the Blessed Virgin. They also distributed fliers in which they protested against "the shameful speculation that has been made from the ridiculous comedy in Fatima."

The demonstration was not successful. Many people, including those who did not believe in the apparitions, were filled with indignation at their vulgar actions. City officials, though, pretended that they neither saw nor knew what was going on, thereby condoning this sacrilegious event.

The newspapers printed protests. Some Catholics banded together and sent an open letter to the authorities. The three visionaries were deeply saddened by the news, and they went immediately to Cova da Iria to see for themselves.

To their great delight, they realized that the thieves had cut down the wrong holm oak. The little tree over which Mary stood was still there, although faithful believers had already stripped it of its branches and leaves and reduced it to a little trunk that could hardly be seen. It is for this reason, perhaps, that it escaped the ax of the sacrilegious bandits.

"Touched" by the Supernatural

With the end to the apparitions, the three visionaries remained alone and abandoned. They needed a spiritual director, but none of the priests in the area dared to get involved, fearing disciplinary sanctions from their superiors, who were suspicious of visions, miracles, and other similar things.

In reality, ecclesiastical authorities had already given orders that an investigation be conducted. They had entrusted several priests, who were particularly knowledgeable in the area, with the task of examining, questioning, and evaluating the facts. Since these priests were responsible for acting as judges, they could not serve as "spiritual fathers" to the children. Thus, Lucia, Francisco, and Jacinta were left to their own devices.

Fortunately, they demonstrated maturity and a balance that few people of their age could claim.

"Obviously," Fr. Valinho said, "Mary continued to take care of them. She no longer appeared, but she was always with them and guided them with her maternal care. She had entrusted a mission to them—a mission that would be short for Francisco and Jacinta, but long for Lucia.

"She had asked the children to pray and make sacrifices for the conversion of sinners, and they did so very generously. Only Lucia knows to what extent they prayed, sacrificed, and did penance in order to carry out Mary's wish. She has told about some things, but there are certainly many other things that she has kept hidden in her heart."

"Were there visible signs of their dedication to prayer?"

"Thanks to their constant union with God, the three children received God's blessing and carried it wherever they went. They were fonts of heavenly graces. They radiated faith, peace, hope, light, and optimism to all those who came in contact with them.

"At times only their physical presence was enough to resolve painful situations and attract the Lord's blessing. There are numerous, inexplicable episodes that took place at that time in which they were involved. My mother, my grandmother, my aunts and uncles, and many other eyewitnesses have testified to this."

"Can you tell us some of their stories?"

"There truly are many of them, but I can mention some of the more significant ones. One day Lucia learned from her sister, my Aunt Teresa, that the son of one of their friends had been arrested and thrown in jail, accused of a serious crime. The young man said he was innocent.

"Teresa was very sad and asked Lucia to pray to Mary so that people would realize that the young man was innocent. Lucia was disturbed by what her sister told her. The next morning, on her way to school, she told her cousins, Francisco and Jacinta.

"When they reached the parish church where they always stopped to pay a visit to the 'Hidden Jesus,' Francisco said, 'I'm not going to school today. I'm going to stay here and pray that the innocence of that young man will be recognized.' When school was over, Lucia went back to the church and Francisco was still there.

" 'Did you pray?' she asked him.

" 'Yes,' Francisco answered. 'You can tell your sister that the young man will be free.'

"A few days later the young man was set free because people realized he was innocent."

The "Blessings" of Francisco and Jacinta

"On another occasion," Fr. Valinho continued, "a woman stopped the three children in the street. 'I'm very sick,' the poor woman said. 'I can't provide for my family. I have little children. Ask the Blessed Virgin to heal me.'

"She knelt in the middle of the street and sobbed. Jacinta went up to her and reached for her hands in an effort to console her, but the woman refused to get up. So Jacinta knelt down in front of her.

" 'Let's pray together,' she told her. They recited the Hail Mary three times. Then Jacinta added, 'I will continue to pray, and Mary will surely heal you.' From that day on, Jacinta remembered that poor woman in her prayers. After a few weeks, the woman returned to thank the Blessed Virgin because she was completely healed."

"We don't want to take too much advantage of your patience, but can you tell us another one of these extraordinary stories?"

"Gladly. One day when they were on their way to pray the rosary at Cova da Iria, Lucia, Francisco, and Jacinta met a young man who was lying on the ground and crying at the site of the apparitions.

" 'Don't cry, Mary is so good,' Jacinta told him. She was a very sensitive soul, and was always moved to tears by other people's suffering.

" 'I have to do my military service,' the young man explained. 'But I'm married and have a little baby boy. My wife is sick and cannot take care of him anymore. Pray for me. Ask Mary either to heal my wife or to have my call-up temporarily revoked.'

" 'We'll pray,' the three children answered. 'The Blessed Virgin will surely bless you.'

"A few months went by and the young man returned. He had his baby in his arms and his wife at his side. His face was radiant.

" 'I received two blessings,' he said. 'On the eve of my departure for the army, I came down with a terrible fever, so they excused me from doing my military service. In the meantime, my wife was completely healed of her illness. Now we are a happy family, and we've come to thank the Blessed Virgin.' "

"Did you personally know any of these people who were blessed with a miracle?"

"There are many people whom I know personally who have told me about blessings they have received from Francisco and Jacinta while they were still alive. I always marvel at these stories. In my opinion, it's only natural that the Blessed Virgin would be ready to answer the prayers of these children, who showed so much love and devotion for her."

"Distracted" by Jesus

Francisco and Jacinta were able to obtain blessings from heaven with their prayers, but few people paid attention to them here on earth. Despite the fact that many people considered them to be "little saints," church authorities looked upon them with suspicion.

Francisco, for example, had not yet been allowed to make his first Holy Communion.

He desired to do so very much. He envied Lucia, who could frequently draw near to the "table of the angels." Whenever his cousin returned from Mass, he used to kiss her heart, saying, "Jesus is there." He remembered very well the mysterious Communion that he had received from the angel! He repeatedly told his family that he desired so much to be allowed to receive the "bread of angels."

Every so often, his father, Manuel Marto, spoke to the pastor of the parish about this, but the pastor was convinced that Francisco was not ready. "Let's wait," he always answered.

His suspicion was rooted in an incident that had occurred a few months earlier. Francisco and Jacinta were attending catechism with other children their age, so that they could make their first Communion. It was during the apparitions. Jacinta followed the lessons attentively, but Francisco was often distracted.

From the moment the apparitions began, Francisco had little interest in what was happening around him. He had become a contemplative. He liked to be alone. Even when he was in the pasture with the sheep, he would leave Lucia and Jacinta and hide in some grotto. "I pray and think about Jesus," he told Lucia, who would look for him and scold him for his behavior.

Of the various recommendations that the Blessed Virgin had made during those months, the one that had remained especially engraved in his heart was the call to pray for the reparation of men's sins against Jesus. He was tormented by the thought that Jesus was sad and suffering. He had a burning desire to console him. Even while he was at his catechism lesson, he was distracted because he was thinking about Jesus and about the joy of finally receiving him in his own heart.

These thoughts were so strong that he often did not even hear the priest when he called on him. The priest was worried. When the course was finished, Jacinta passed, but Francisco failed. "He's not ready because he doesn't know his catechism," he told Manuel Marto curtly.

This was a terrible blow for Francisco. For a long time he cried and could not be consoled. Finally, he said, "I'll offer up this suffering to the Lord. He knows that I love him very much."

The Center of Curiosity

"I believe that being excluded from making his first Communion with his sister caused enormous suffering for Francisco," Fr. Valinho said. "He was a sensitive but shy boy. He carried that pain within him; thus it became even greater.

"He probably cried many tears as he watched Jacinta make her first Communion, while he was unable to join her. From the moment that the apparitions began, the three children were constantly plagued by problems. It seemed as though the forces of evil were unleashed against them as revenge for the privilege of seeing the Virgin Mary. There were constant pain and adversity, even when the apparitions were no longer happening. In fact, the pain and adversity increased."

"Then there were all the curious people," we observed.

"Of course. The three children enjoyed no peace. Everyone wanted to get to know them, talk to them, question them, and check them out. They felt it was their obligation to doubt and to judge.

"Lucia, Francisco, and Jacinta were the focus of people's curiosity, and this upset their lives and their families' lives. Every word and every deed led to gossip, inferences, and suppositions that, in turn, caused misunderstandings and tension. They were held responsible for all the confusion and all the inconvenience that disturbed the tranquil existence of their families and the people of Fatima.

"Often priests came who said they were sent by the bishop but who were really only curious and wanted to trick the children into making contradictory statements. The children trusted them when they interrogated them because they were men of the Church, but these sessions ended up becoming painful inquisitions. Lucia and Jacinta often succeeded in getting away. Francisco was more naive and was easy prey for these pitiless people."

"We also know that your grandmother, Lucia's mother, got sick at that time."

"Quite seriously. My mother, who was the oldest of the daughters and felt responsible for the whole family, was very worried. She got angry with Lucia and said, 'It's your fault. You and your lies have reduced mother to this state.'

"Lucia cried. The situation was getting worse and worse. At one point, there was no longer any hope for my grandmother. People gave up, and everyone thought she was going to die at any minute.

"Finally, my mother's desperation reached a peak. After having bitterly scolded Lucia once again, she added, 'If you really did see the Madonna, go to Cova da Iria and pray. Don't come back unless the Virgin Mary grants you the blessing of mother's healing.' "

A Mysterious Healing

Poor Lucia left the house crying. She was shattered. Her morale was at ground zero. Because of her sister's unrelenting psychological hammering, she was convinced that she was responsible for her mother's condition. She went to Cova da Iria. When she arrived at the site of the apparitions, she knelt down and poured out all her suffering.

"Mary must have had mercy on her favorite daughter," Fr. Valinho commented. "She probably said something to her, but we don't know for sure. We do know that when she returned home, she discovered that her mother was well. She had been healed. She got out of bed and didn't feel any more pain.

"My grandmother lived for many more years. As a sign of thanksgiving to Mary, Lucia returned to Cova da Iria for nine consecutive days to pray. At the end of the novena, my grandmother joined her because she knew that her sudden healing was really miraculous.

"There was another problem that tormented the three visionaries during that time," Fr. Valinho said after a brief pause. "It concerned the construction of the chapel at the site of the apparitions that the Blessed Virgin had requested. Maria Carreira was collecting the people's offerings, and she jealously guarded the money. She constantly asked the people to heed Mary's request, but the civil authorities were against the idea, and the pastor of the parish didn't want to get involved.

"Rumors were circulating that the parents of the children, and even Maria Carreira herself, were spending the money. The mayor of Vila Nova de Ourem asked that an investigation be conducted and decided to sue Mrs. Carreira's husband. All these malicious actions weighed heavily on the poor hearts of the three children.

"Fortunately, people finally decided to build the chapel without waiting for permission from the authorities. My grandfather, who owned the land, gave his consent. A bricklayer was hired, and his son helped him. Thus, the first chapel was constructed. When people tried to have it blessed, all the priests refused to do so. No one wanted to get involved in the whole matter."

"What suspicion!"

"The worse thing is that this mistrust and meanness only created suffering and anxiety for the three children. They offered these sacrifices and this humiliation to the Lord, but they suffered a lot. The bricklayer who built the chapel and who was a good Christian saw all these problems.

" 'If this is the work of God, we're only beginning our suffering,' he commented. He was right. The forces of evil always stand in the way of God's work, wanting to destroy it."

18

FRANCISCO'S DEATH

During the second apparition on June 13, the Blessed Virgin told Lucia, "I will soon come to take Francisco and Jacinta with me to heaven, but you, Lucia, must remain here below."

Francisco and Jacinta often recalled this word. They considered it a wonderful promise. Whenever they faced the danger of death, they said joyfully, "Now we're going to heaven." Their experience of the apparitions was so sublime and so exhilarating that they desired death as a way of more quickly achieving that state of happiness and bliss that the Blessed Virgin had allowed them to see.

One day a woman asked Francisco, "What do you want to be when you grow up?"

"Nothing. I'm going to die soon and go to heaven," was his immediate response.

"But if you don't die, would you like to be a carpenter?" the woman asked once again.

"No," Francisco answered.

"Would you like to join the army and become a captain so you can head up a big division and command the soldiers?"

"No," Francisco said.

"Well, then," the woman continued, "do you dream about studying and becoming a lawyer or a doctor so you can heal the sick and save many lives?"

"No," the boy repeated.

"You've been very fortunate to see the Blessed Virgin," the woman continued. "Certainly you would like to dedicate your life to God and become a priest so that you might serve souls."

"No," Francisco said decisively.

The woman looked at him with a look of dismay. She did not understand his attitude. "So then, what do you want to do when you're grown up?"

"Nothing," Francisco answered candidly. "I don't want to be anything and I don't want to do anything. I wish to die soon and go to heaven. The Blessed Virgin promised it to me."

The Arrival of the "Spanish Flu"

Francisco was a young boy of few words but with a quick mind. He knew that Mary would have never made a promise without keeping it. He had complete faith in her.

Never, even for a short instant, did he doubt, not even when Lucia no longer wanted to keep their appointments, feeling that they might be Satan's tricks. He was the one who convinced his cousin to change her mind and to return to Cova da Iria. He considered Mary's words, "I shall soon come to take Francisco and Jacinta with me to heaven," to be prophetic, and he impatiently awaited their fulfillment.

At the end of October 1918 he became ill. The Spanish influenza was raging throughout Portugal, a horrible flu that originated in Spain and later spread throughout Europe and the rest of the world, causing more than twenty million deaths within a short time. Francisco and Jacinta both caught it, as well as their mother and all their brothers and sisters. Only their father, Manuel Marto, remained healthy and was able to care for the entire family.

The epidemic was serious. The flu caused high fevers and tremendous exhaustion. Nevertheless, Francisco and Jacinta were not afraid. They knew their lives were already drawing to an end, and they joyfully accepted their fate. The illness was a sign to them that the Blessed Mother's promise was about to come true.

"Francisco's illness lasted almost six months," Fr. Valinho said. "It came and went, so he had his good days and his bad days. Every so often, the boy would feel better, get out of bed, and find the strength to go to Cova da Iria to pray the rosary.

"Then he would have a relapse, and each one was more serious than the previous time. At a certain point, the illness affected his lungs, probably causing bronchial pneumonia. Francisco knew he was slowly growing worse, but he never complained."

"Has Sr. Lucia said anything to you about her cousin's illness?"

"My aunt said that Francisco always seemed happy throughout his illness. She would visit him every day, and sometimes even two or three times a day."

" 'Do you suffer very much?' she asked him.

" 'Very much,' he answered. 'But it doesn't matter. I'm suffering to console our Lord and then, after a while, I'm going to heaven.'

" 'When you're there, don't forget about me. Ask Mary to come and take me.'

" 'No, I can't do that. You know very well that the Blessed Virgin doesn't want you there yet. You must remain here to spread devotion to her Immaculate Heart.' "

At the beginning of 1919, his illness grew worse. Francisco could no longer get out of bed. It was then that the Virgin Mary appeared to him.

He was in bed, and Jacinta was keeping him company. The Blessed Virgin appeared to him at the foot of his bed. She said that she would soon be coming to take him. She would return shortly for Jacinta.

"Did Francisco recount this vision?" we asked.

"No, Jacinta told Lucia about it. 'Our Lady came to save us,' the little girl said. 'She said that she would soon come to take Francisco. She asked me if I was willing to pray for the conversion of many more sinners, and I told her that I was.

" 'Mary wants me to go to two different hospitals, but not to get well. I will suffer more for love for God, for the conversion of sinners, and in reparation for the offenses that have been committed against her Immaculate Heart. She told me that you wouldn't go with me. My mother will accompany me to the hospital, but then I'll be alone, and I'll die alone.' "

An Extraordinary Attraction

"Francisco's conduct throughout his illness," Fr. Valinho said, "was exemplary. Everyone who had contact with him during that time was deeply impressed by his goodness, serenity, and holiness. He lay in bed silently and patiently. He prayed constantly.

"My Aunt Olimpia, Francisco's mother, told me that he never complained. For him everything was just fine. He took whatever was offered to him. He even drank the bitterest medicine without complaining. Since he never complained, everyone thought he would be healed. Although his illness was relentless and his body was wasting away, his suffering probably stirred him on."

"Who saw him during his illness?"

"Many children from the neighboring houses visited him and spoke to him through the window. They wanted to know whether he was feeling better. When they asked him whether he wanted one of them to stay with him and keep him company, he said he preferred to be by himself. Then he said to Lucia, 'I prefer it when only you and Jacinta are here.'

"There were many adults who visited him, but Francisco was always silent in their presence. He only spoke if they asked him a question, and answered with very few words. He was shy.

"But even if he rarely spoke, people were attracted to him. Aunt Olimpia told me that, after visiting Francisco, many of her friends commented, 'Entering that room, I felt like I was entering a church. It felt so good to be near him. I experienced a deep interior peace.' "

"Is there any special story from that time in his life that illustrates one of those 'blessings' that the shepherd children seemed to bestow?" we asked our patient guide.

"One day, when he was near death, a certain woman named Marianna came to see him. She came because her husband had thrown one of their sons out of the house. The woman asked for the grace that her husband and her son might be reconciled.

"Francisco answered, 'Don't worry. Soon I'll be going to heaven, and when I arrive there, I'll ask Mary for this grace.'

"The evening of the day when Francisco died, the son returned home and asked his father for forgiveness. The two men were reconciled, and peace was restored to their home. The sister of that young man, who was named Leocadia, later married one of Francisco and Jacinta's brothers."

Communion at Last

"The child was afraid that he would die before making his first Communion," Fr. Valinho told us after a brief pause. "Every so often he would tell his father how much he wished to be able to receive the 'bread of angels.' Manuel Marto told the parish priest, who always said, 'The boy is not prepared.'

"Uncle Manuel suffered because of this, but he, too, had a certain fear of the parish priest and dared not contradict him. Francisco grew worse at the beginning of April 1919. He grew tired simply from breathing, because his lungs were filled with fluid. Seeing his health deteriorate so much, Uncle Manuel decided to speak once again to the parish priest.

The priest wasn't there that day. There was another priest who was filling in for him. Upon learning about Francisco's condition, he offered to stop by the following day to hear Francisco's confession and bring him Communion."

"Francisco must have been delighted!"

"Very much. Right away he sent his sister Teresa to fetch Lucia. When Lucia arrived, he told her, 'Tomorrow I'll go to confession and then I'll die. I want you to help me make a good confession. You have to tell me if you ever saw me committing any sins.'

"Lucia thought for a moment and answered, 'You've disobeyed your mother. Sometimes she's told you to stay in the house and you ran away to play with me.'

" 'You're right,' Francisco said. 'I've made Jesus suffer because of my disobedience. I'll confess that sin and hope that the Lord will forgive me. Now go find Jacinta and ask her if she remembers any of my sins.'

"Jacinta, who was also in bed with the flu, sent him a message telling him that he had stolen some money from José Marto at Casa Velha before the apparitions, and that he had thrown some stones at the children from some nearby houses.

" 'Yes, that's true,' Francisco said. 'I've sinned much, but the Lord is good and he'll forgive me.'

"He went to confession. Then the priest quizzed him on his catechism. Uncle Manuel was afraid that Francisco would fail because he was so weak. He hardly had any breath to speak. However, the child's answers were satisfactory.

" 'Tomorrow I'll bring you Communion,' the priest finally said. Francisco's eyes filled with tears."

Time to Go to Heaven

"What did Francisco experience that day?" we asked Fr. Valinho.

"We don't know. He certainly confided in Lucia, but she's never been willing to share anything. Knowing how much Francisco lovingly awaited that encounter, you can imagine that his happiness was overwhelming.

"Now he felt he was ready. The end was near. The next day, April 3, Lucia lingered by Francisco's bedside until it was late. Every so often she asked him if he was suffering. 'Yes,' he said in a faint voice, 'but all my suffering is for the love of the Lord and of the Blessed Virgin.'

"Taking advantage of a moment when his mother left the room, Francisco asked Lucia for the rope that he wore as a penance, saying, 'Take it away before my mother sees it. Now I no longer run the risk of having it for the rest of my life.' He didn't even have the energy to pray. He asked Lucia and Jacinta to pray the rosary next to his bed, while he prayed mentally."

"Were those his last words?"

"No. Before his passing away that evening, Lucia said, 'Goodbye, Francisco. If you go to heaven during the night, don't forget about me down here.'

" 'Don't worry, I won't forget you,' he answered.

"Lucia said that he held her right hand and squeezed it for a while. He looked at her with tears in his eyes.

" 'Do you want something else?' Lucia asked.

" 'No.'

"Lucia left. The following day, Friday, April 4, at about ten o'clock in the morning, Francisco whispered to his mother, who was at his side: 'Mama, look at the beautiful light, there by the window.' He was silent but he smiled, as though he could see something. Then he said, 'Now I don't see it anymore.'

"After a moment, he breathed his last breath with a tremble but without a groan. It was as though he fell asleep. He was ten years and almost ten months old."

"What did his parents say?"

"His father said, 'He died smiling.' Aunt Olimpia said, 'He smiled and continued to smile, without breathing.'

"The funeral Mass was celebrated the following day, on April 5. It was a simple funeral, and hardly anyone accompanied his body to the cemetery because the Spanish flu was still raging and many people were sick in bed. He was buried in the small parish cemetery. His grave was marked by a small cross, and it was no different from the other graves."

19

THE LITTLE MARTYR

Jacinta could not accompany her brother's coffin to the cemetery, because she was in bed with a high fever. Francisco's suffering had come to an end, but her Calvary would last for another eleven months.

Jacinta's illness began when she contracted the Spanish influenza in October 1918. Her condition worsened, and there were other complications. It was only later, when she was confined to a hospital in Lisbon where some prominent specialists were able to examine her, that an exact report on her condition was possible.

According to several prominent physicians, she suffered from "purulent, fistulous pleurisy of the left large cavity, and osteitis of the seventh and eighth ribs on the same side." Their curt, dry language conveyed a serious diagnosis.

By the time Francisco died in April 1919, little Jacinta could no longer stand on her own. She was pale and frail. She spent days in her room, immersed in prayer. Lucia's visits were her only comfort. Several times during the day, when Lucia was returning home from school or when she took a break from her work at home, she would go and spend a little time with Jacinta.

The two cousins spent a lot of time alone in her room, praying together and confiding in each other.

Lucia was in good health. The Spanish flu had not affected her. However, she was saddened by the fact that members of her family were sick. The terrible influenza also struck her father, Antonio dos Santos, and it caused some other related problems from which he would not recover.

Two Months in the Hospital

During the months of May and June, both Jacinta's and Antonio dos Santos' health grew worse. Lucia divided her time between her father's and her cousin's beds. Then, toward the end of June, Manuel Marto decided to send his daughter to the hospital of San Agostinho in Vila Nova de Ourem.

Shortly after entering the hospital, Jacinta told Lucia, "Now I only have a little time left before I go to heaven. You will remain here to tell people that God wants to establish devotion to the Immaculate Heart of Mary throughout the world. When you have the opportunity to do so, don't hide. Tell everybody that God gives us grace through the Immaculate Heart of Mary, that they should ask her for it, and that the heart of Jesus wants the Immaculate Heart of Mary to be venerated next to his."

Lucia brought her cousin a picture of Jesus' heart. "How ugly," Jacinta said when she looked at it. "It doesn't at all resemble the Lord who is so beautiful! But I still want this picture." She kept it under her pillow and she frequently kissed it, saying, "I kiss him on his heart, which is what pleases me the most."

A few days later she told Lucia, "Oh, if you only had a picture of Mary's heart! Do you have one? I would love to have both together." Lucia was able to fulfill her request, and Jacinta was delighted.

She entered the hospital in Vila Nova de Ourem on July 1, 1919. She made the trip on a donkey, accompanied by her father. The doctors wanted her to undergo some special treatments in order to treat a large wound that had formed in her chest, probably due to the fistulas from the pleurisy.

Jacinta remained there for two months. But she felt worse and was lonely. Her family members were unable to visit her because of other illnesses in the family, and Lucia's father was dying. Antonio dos Santos died at the end of July. Only then was Lucia able to visit her cousin and share with her the sorrow of losing her father.

"Lucia," Fr. Valinho explained, "was very attached to her father. My grandfather, who seemed so gruff, was really a sensitive person. He loved his daughter very much, and as we've noted before, when my grandmother scolded her, he would take her in his arms, leave the house, go out to the fields, and hold her close. That way he let her know that he loved her dearly and was protecting her.

"Lucia sensed that her father believed what she was saying, and, for this reason, she had a special affection for him. When her father died, Lucia felt tremendously alone. She loved her mother and her sisters very much, but she knew that they did not believe what was happening to her and that they considered her a liar. For this reason she could not count on their support and was unable to confide in them. Her only true friend was Jacinta, and she clung to her even more."

"Did she visit her in the hospital?" we asked Fr. Valinho.

"In the month of August 1919, Lucia went to the hospital on two occasions, accompanied by my Aunt Olimpia. The two cousins hugged each other joyfully. Jacinta asked her mother to leave them alone.

"Lucia asked her whether she was suffering, and Jacinta answered, 'I'm suffering a lot, but I'm offering it all to the Lord for the conversion of sinners and in reparation for offenses to the Immaculate Heart of Mary. I like suffering out of love for Jesus and for the Blessed Virgin. They very much love those who suffer for the conversion of sinners.'

"Unfortunately, Jacinta's stay in the hospital was of no avail. Moreover, the expenses were too high, and after two months, Manuel Marto was forced to take his daughter home."

"I'll Die Alone"

"Jacinta's visits with Lucia," Fr. Valinho continued, "returned to their daily schedule. The two children spent a good amount of time together. Whenever they were alone, they would talk. But if someone arrived, they lowered their voices and interrupted their conversation.

"Their mothers were intrigued by their behavior, especially Lucia's mother. 'When you're alone,' she noted, 'you talk nonstop and you try not to miss a word, even if someone is overhearing. But as soon as someone enters the room, you lower your heads and don't say another word. I can't understand this mystery.'"

"Was it really a mystery?" we asked inquisitively.

"In her memoirs, Lucia alludes to her mother's and her aunt's curiosity. She says that her conversations with Jacinta during this period of her illness centered on their memories of everything that had happened. They recalled the apparitions, Mary's words, the promises they received, and also the secret. They discussed the content of the 'secret' but were careful so that no one would overhear.

"As I noted before, one day Jacinta told Lucia that the Blessed Virgin had visited her again. She had revealed to Jacinta that after entering a second hospital, she wouldn't see Lucia or even her parents again. After much suffering, she would die alone. Mary had also told Jacinta not to be afraid, because she would come to take her to heaven."

"How did Jacinta react to this revelation?"

"She was sad. The idea of dying alone scared her. 'I won't see you again,' she repeated to Lucia. 'You won't be able to visit me in Lisbon, and I'll die alone.'

" 'Don't think about it,' Lucia said.

" 'Let me think about it,' Jacinta answered, 'because the more I think about it, the more I suffer. I want to suffer out of love for the Lord and for sinners.' "

"Is Sr. Lucia the only witness to Jacinta's great desire to suffer out of love for Jesus?"

"No. There are numerous witnesses," Fr. Valinho said. "Many other people have attested to this. Her illness, which caused piercing pains, often brought her to tears. But she had learned that pain is mysteriously useful in the economy of salvation, and she sought after it.

"For her, pain had become like an expression of love. For this reason, she no longer complained. When you consider that her illness, which included a wound in her chest that was eating her alive, was a genuine Calvary that lasted months and months, you can see how she behaved like a real martyr—a little one, but a great one. It is her holiness in the way of living out this suffering that the Church recognizes today."

A New Hope

Jacinta's condition grew worse. The wound in her chest grew larger and was now visible to the naked eye. The little girl needed medicine on a daily basis, but Aljustrel lacked nurses and adequate health care materials for such delicate care.

Around the middle of January 1920, Jacinta received a surprise visit. Rev. Formigão, to whom the Cardinal of Lisbon had entrusted the task of following the events concerning the apparitions in Fatima, came to visit her with his friend, a professor by the name of Eurico Lisboa.

This time, however, Rev. Formigão did not come to question the little girl again. Knowing that Jacinta was gravely ill, he wanted his friend, an illustrious physician from Lisbon, to examine her.

Rev. Formigão believed in the apparitions and was convinced they were genuine. For this reason, he was concerned about the visionary's health. He had confided his feelings about the events in Fatima to his doctor friend. He, too, was excited about them and wanted to meet Jacinta, hoping to be useful in some way in her recovery.

Dr. Lisboa visited Jacinta and realized that her condition was very serious. The child's family informed him that the doctors at the hospital in Vila Nova de Ourem had said that they could do nothing for her.

"That's not true," the doctor protested. "You should never lose hope. You have to do everything possible. Wherever there's life, there's hope. You shouldn't resign yourselves to the worst."

"We've spent almost all our resources paying for hospitals," Manuel Marto said. "When they told us they could no longer do anything, we brought her home. As you can see, we also have two other daughters who are very sick, and we have to take care of them, too."

Dr. Lisboa insisted that they should try another course of treatment. He offered to speak to his colleagues in Lisbon to find a way of caring for Jacinta at a large hospital in the city.

"It's so far," the girl's father said. But Rev. Formigão advised them to try once again. So the decision was made. Jacinta would go to Lisbon.

When he returned to the capital, Dr. Lisboa arranged for her care. On January 21, Jacinta left by train, accompanied by her mother.

Lisbon

Before leaving Fatima, Jacinta asked if someone could take her one more time to Cova da Iria. Her mother asked a friend to lend her a donkey, and she took the child to the site of the apparitions. On the way there, Jacinta wanted to get down from the donkey so she could gather some flowers to take to the little chapel, which had just been completed.

She knelt down next to the remains of the holm oak where the Blessed Virgin had stood, and prayed for a long time. She knew that she would never see the place again. She looked around, as though she wanted to engrave in her memory every little detail. She spent a long time examining every little detail of the chapel, and returned home in the evening on the back of the donkey.

Lucia stopped by to see her for the last time. They hugged each other and wept together. Lucia said, "She hugged me around the neck for a long time, and crying, she told me, 'We won't see each other again. Pray for me constantly, until I get to heaven. When I am there, I shall pray for you without stopping. Never tell the secret to anyone, even though they want to kill you. Love Jesus and the Immaculate Heart of Mary, and make sacrifices for sinners.' "

On the train to Lisbon, Jacinta stood by the window the whole time. She was enchanted by the countryside.

In the capital, she was offered hospitality at the orphanage of Our Lady of Miracles. The superior and foundress of the institute, Maria Purificação Godinho, immediately realized the depth of her spirituality, and the two became good friends. Jacinta called the nun "godmother" and confided in her. The sister treated her like a daughter and was close to her.

Jacinta spent ten days at the orphanage. She was happy because she could see the old Chapel of Miracles from a balcony. From that vantage point, she could also see the tabernacle in the church. Jacinta asked someone to take her there each day. There she prayed and thought about Jesus.

The wound in her chest was dreadful. It gave off an unbearable odor. The infection was spreading more and more. The pain was surely atrocious, but the little girl bore it with marvelous courage and resignation.

"Many people were fooled by the fact that Jacinta didn't complain," Fr. Valinho said. "They underestimated the tremendous pains she had. From testimonies by Dr. Lisboa and Mother Godinho, in whom Jacinta confided, we know that her pain was terrible and unrelenting, and continuing day and night. We also know that the child never complained.

"Dr. Lisboa was convinced that he could still save Jacinta. He was intent on doing so and referred her to his illustrious colleague, Professor Castro Freire, one of the most highly esteemed pediatricians in Portugal, who worked at the Doña Stefania Hospital."

"What did the doctors decide?"

"After a consultation together, they decided to operate in order to eliminate the infection that had spread in her chest. Aunt Olimpia did not agree with them. She didn't want her little girl to undergo such martyrdom, but they were finally able to convince her. However, she couldn't stay for the operation. Her other children were sick at home, and she was needed there. Thus, Jacinta remained alone just as the Blessed Mother had said."

"Oh, Mary, It Hurts"

"The little girl was hospitalized on February 2," Fr. Valinho recounted. "Her bed was number 38. Right away she felt sick. The atmosphere was typical of hospitals. The personnel were cold and distant, and she suffered tremendously because she was so sensitive. Fortunately, Mother Godinho visited her every day.

"They operated on her on February 10. It was a very delicate and painful surgery. Since she was so weak and run down, she could not endure total anesthesia. Therefore, they used a local anesthesia, and she truly suffered like a martyr. They removed two ribs from the left side of her thorax. The wound was so large, a hand could fit into it."

"The pain must have really been atrocious," we commented.

"It was sheer agony when she had to take her medication. 'Oh, Mary, it hurts,' she mumbled through her teeth. However, the Blessed Virgin did not forget her, and every so often would go and console her.

"Mother Godinho revealed this fact. 'The day after the surgery, I was sitting on the edge of her bed and she said, "Not there, Mother, because the Blessed Virgin is there." ' "

"Was the surgery a success?"

"It seemed to be. But really it served no purpose. It only made the little martyr suffer more."

February 20 was a Friday. In the evening, Jacinta said that she felt sick and wished to have the sacraments. A priest from the neighboring Church of the Angels was summoned, and he heard her confession. Jacinta asked if she might receive the viaticum, but he felt she did not seem in danger of dying. "I'll bring it tomorrow," he said and left.

"Jacinta was mortified," Fr. Valinho said. "She said so to a nurse, a young girl by the name of Aurora, with whom she had become friends. Crying, she told her that she shouldn't die abandoned by everyone and without holding Jesus to her heart.

"Even Aurora thought the child was exaggerating and wasn't concerned enough to stay nearby. But a little later, around 10:30 P.M., she realized that Jacinta was no longer breathing. She died, alone, without being able to receive Communion. Her funeral was held the next day at noon. Her dress, white with a blue bow, just as Jacinta wanted, was a gift from two women in Lisbon."

"And her parents?"

"Her mother and father couldn't attend. They didn't know where to bury her, but Dr. Lisboa had sensed the child's holiness and said that it would be fine to bury her in a special niche, until the matter of the apparitions was clarified. He suggested that they bury her in the Church of the Angels, but the pastor of the church was opposed.

"In the meantime, the casket with Jacinta's body was taken to a corner in the sacristy, and people immediately noticed something out of the ordinary. News about her death had spread through the city, and people who wanted to pay their respects to her body started to arrive. It was an unending procession.

"The parish pastor was worried and feared what the chancery office would say. He had her body moved to a room above the sacristy, and people came for two days nonstop to view her body."

Tribute at the Shrine

Upon receiving word of Jacinta's death, Baron di Alvaiàzere, one of the first people to support the authenticity of the apparitions at Fatima, offered a family tomb at the cemetery of Vila Nova de Ourem. Public health laws stipulated that the body had to be enclosed in a zinc casket in order to be transported there. Her body was transferred from the oak casket to the zinc one on the morning of February 24.

Jacinta had already been dead for four days. Her body, which had been eaten away by her purulent sores, should have given off an unbearable stench. Instead, the people present, including the public health authorities, noticed that it smelled like the sweet perfume of flowers.

That afternoon, her second funeral took place in Ourem. It was raining, but a large crowd was present.

"Jacinta's father came to the funeral and cried like a baby," Fr. Valinho told us. "Jacinta remained in that tomb until September 12, 1935, when her body was transferred to the cemetery in Fatima to a new tomb that had been specially prepared for her and her brother, Francisco. On May 1, 1951, her body was taken to the Basilica, and the following year Francisco's body was also moved to the shrine.

"The two visionaries are now buried there, as you've already seen. But let's go see their tomb one more time," Fr. Valinho said spontaneously and enthusiastically. "Let's go pay our respects to the bodies of these two little but great saints, Mary's favorites."

We arrived at the large piazza in front of the shrine. Fr. Valinho walked quickly toward the church. We walked up the long staircase and entered.

Before our eyes was a sight that we had seen several times in the past few days, but that has never ceased to amaze us. The tombs of the two children are in small chapels adjacent to the main altar. Francisco's tomb is to the right and Jacinta's to the left.

Even though it was evening and the flow of pilgrims had tapered off compared to other hours during the day, two lines of people that extended the length of the church were waiting to visit the two tombs. The people walked slowly, devoutly, and orderly. There were men and women, teenagers and small children, as well as people from every nation and of every race. They stopped for a few seconds in front of the tombs, prayed, and then moved on so that those who were waiting could take their place.

"It's always like this—every day of the year and at every hour of the day," Fr. Valinho whispered. "It's incredible to see the affection that these people show for the children. Even I, who come here very often, feel an attraction that never diminishes."

His eyes were shining with emotion. We stood in line with him and made our way to the tombs where the remains of the two children are kept. Even though they have been dead for many years, we realized that they are more alive than ever.

"We'll Go to Coimbra"

When we left, it was already getting dark. The large, empty piazza seemed immense in the dim, ethereal light.

"Our trip has come to an end," we said to Fr. Valinho. He looked at us and smiled.

"Tomorrow, I, too, will return home. It's Saturday. I have responsibilities at the parish."

"You have been very kind to us, and we don't know how to thank you."

"I'm happy that I was able to be of service. I'm very interested in making known the story of Fatima and of the three visionaries."

"What time are you leaving tomorrow?"

"I don't know. There are several trains from Fatima to Oporto. I haven't decided which one to take."

"No, not a train. We'll meet you tomorrow morning and drive you home in our car."

"But Oporto is quite far."

"That doesn't matter. We're happy to do so because we also want to ask one last, big favor."

"What is it?"

"You have to introduce Sr. Lucia to us. We know that it's almost impossible to get near your aunt, but after having spoken with Francisco and Jacinta's brother, with the woman who was healed, and with the nieces and nephews of the visionaries, we would very much like it, even if we could only see Sr. Lucia."

Fr. Valinho broke out in a hearty laugh.

"Dear friends, I would gladly do so, but it's impossible," he said. "Sr. Lucia cannot speak with anyone. First of all, she is a cloistered nun, which means that she is in a 'living tomb,' as they used to say. She cannot have any contact with the outside world.

"Secondly, there are explicit instructions from the Vatican regarding contact with her. No person can speak with Sr. Lucia unless that person has written permission, first of all, from the Holy See—that is, the pope. Bishops, cardinals, and other ecclesiastical authorities can actually visit a cloistered monastery and speak with the nuns, but not with Sr. Lucia. Very special permission is needed to see her."

"But why are there such rigid restrictions about seeing her?"

"To spare her from curiosity. Because of the apparitions, and especially because of the famous third secret, she has always been the center of intense curiosity. The Holy See has issued these directives so she can live in peace."

Sr. Lucia is the key personality of the apparitions of Fatima. To be there in Portugal, with her nephew, a few miles from where she lives, stirred up a great desire in us to have even some little contact with her. Since she is such a powerful symbol and the magnet that has attracted the interest of millions and millions of believers in this century, we felt we had to try.

"So, Father, it's not even possible to talk with Sr. Lucia?" we stubbornly asked one more time.

"Impossible, unless you obtain written permission from the pope."

"But you can go and visit her."

"Yes, I can. The Holy See has given permission for all her direct nieces and nephews to visit her two or three times a year. For me, since I'm a priest, I can see her once a month or even more often."

"Are there any precise days on which you can visit her?"

"No, I can choose whatever day I want."

"Therefore, if we take you to Coimbra tomorrow, can you go and talk with your aunt?"

"Certainly. And I'd love to do so, since we need to pass through Coimbra in order to get to Oporto."

"Would you be able to ask your aunt for us what memories she has of her cousins, Francisco and Jacinta, now that they're about to be beatified?"

"I think I can. My aunt is a very kind person."

"So, tomorrow we'll go to Coimbra?" we asked a little hesitantly one more time.

"Fine," Fr. Valinho confirmed with a smile. "We'll go to Coimbra."

20

LUCIA'S LONG JOURNEY

Coimbra is thirty miles from Fatima. We left at ten o'clock in the morning. As usual, Fr. Valinho proved to be a very pleasant traveling companion, brimming with information.

He told us about Lucia's life as we drove.

"Right after the apparitions, it was difficult for her to live in Fatima," he said. "Every day people came to see her and ask her for prayer. While her cousins were alive, she had someone she could relate to. After they died, though, she felt terribly alone.

"In 1921, Church authorities began to become concerned about Lucia's future. The bishop at that time, the Most Rev. José Alves Correia da Silva, decided to entrust the task of studying the events to a theological commission to determine whether they were genuine. However, they needed complete freedom from any preconditions, and Lucia could be an obstacle. Indeed, her presence could stir up emotions among her followers.

"Therefore, the bishop suggested to Lucia's parents that they send her to a boarding school run by nuns so that she would be far from home. Her parents agreed, and so did Lucia."

"Where did they send her?" we asked.

"The bishop recommended a high school run by the Sisters of St. Dorothy di Vilar. 'However, you have to live there incognito,' the bishop warned Lucia. 'You can't tell anyone where you're going. When you're at the school, you must never tell anyone who you are and you must never talk about the apparitions.' "

"What a difficult request!" we commented.

"Really difficult. Lucia, who had just turned fourteen, probably didn't realize it. She was determined to obey because she was convinced that God manifested his will through her superiors. 'I'll do everything you say,' she told the bishop.

"She returned home and didn't speak about the plan with anyone. On June 18, the day of her departure, she woke up at two o'clock in the morning and, accompanied by her mother and her Uncle Carreira, left Fatima. As they passed nearby Cova da Iria, she wanted to go and make one last visit to the site of the apparitions.

"She prayed the rosary and left. She entered the College of the Sisters of St. Dorothy in Vilar, near Oporto, as a student in the boarding school. She was fourteen years and three months old."

Sister of St. Dorothy for Twenty Years

"Was she already thinking about becoming a nun?" we asked Fr. Valinho.

"Yes, she felt a strong call to a life of prayer. She really wished to become a cloistered nun and devote herself to a contemplative life. But she wasn't very familiar with religious life. She thought that all sisters were alike and differed from each other only because of the religious habits they wore.

"Thus, she stayed with the Sisters of St. Dorothy as a student in their convent school. Living with the sisters, she made her decision to enter that religious congregation. She expressed her desire to the superior, who accepted her.

"In October, 1925, she was sent to Pontevedra in Spain, where the Sisters of St. Dorothy have a convent, and began her postulancy there. The following year she was transferred to Tuy, which is also in Spain, where she finished her postulancy and began the novitiate. She made her profession in religious life on October 3, 1928."

"When did the sisters learn that she was the visionary from Fatima?"

"Many years later. Sr. Lucia lived at Tuy for a long time, then returned to Pontevedra, where she took her solemn vows on October 3, 1934. At that time, the bishop of Leiria publicly revealed her identity.

"In 1937 she returned to Tuy. She remained there until 1946, when the bishop ordered her to return to Portugal. After a short visit to her birthplace to visit the sites of the apparitions once more, she was sent to Casa di Sardao, in the little town of Vila Nova de Gaia."

"How did the decision to enter the Carmelites come about?"

"Evidently she began to experience her old desire of leading a contemplative life once again. Furthermore, after the bishop of Leiria disclosed her true identity, she didn't have a moment of peace. People sought her out because they wanted to see her and speak to her.

"Lucia felt that she could not bear all the commotion much longer and requested permission to change her state in life by leaving the Congregation of the Sisters of St. Dorothy and entering the Carmelites. Following the proper procedure, she informed her confessor, who then spoke to the bishop. Then Lucia had to submit a written request to the pope, who granted her request. Thus, in 1948 she became a Carmelite nun."

A Visit to the Carmelites

"That's Coimbra over there. That's the upper part of the city, the oldest part," Fr. Valinho announced.

The ancient city on top of the hill was in front of us. It was majestic in appearance.

"Coimbra is full of culture," Fr. Valinho continued. "It became the capital of the kingdom of Portugal and seat of the famous *Universidade*, the only university in the entire country until 1911."

Leaving the highway, we crossed the Mondego River and began our ascent to the upper part of town. Within ten minutes, we passed under an old Moorish arch.

"This is the Arco de Almedina," Fr. Valinho said. "In front of us is the old Cathedral of Sè Velha."

The atmosphere in the streets of Coimbra seemed almost unreal. It seemed as if life had stopped in the Middle Ages. The streets were narrow, and some were on a steep incline. Narrow stairways that led to little walks and alleys were everywhere. We felt as though a horseman in armor might suddenly appear out of nowhere.

The Carmelite monastery was in the part of town where the university is located. The building is not old, but it looks rather austere. We parked in front. Fr. Valinho took us on a visit to the little church that is accessible from the outside. He showed us two statues, one of the Sacred Heart and one of the Blessed Virgin, that were made according to the directions given by Sr. Lucia. He also showed us the large grill, beyond which the "living dead" are living.

The sister who was serving as the porter took a message to Sr. Lucia. After a short while, the sister returned to say that Sr. Lucia was waiting for her nephew.

"Remember to ask her something about Francisco and Jacinta. Ask her especially what message their beatification has for modern society.

"All right, I certainly will," Fr. Valinho answered before disappearing into the monastery.

He returned after about an hour. He was smiling and happy. We got into the car and started our drive to Oporto.

So Many Memories

"So, how's your aunt?" we asked.

"She's well. When I asked her how she felt, she said to me, 'How do you want me to feel? Like a woman who's ninety-two years old,' and she laughed heartily. For some time she's been complaining about pain in her legs and about the fact that she can't hold a pen in her hand, but she looks good for her age."

"What does she remember about Francisco and Jacinta?"

"Many things. She enjoyed talking about them. She said that Francisco and Jacinta are always present in her thoughts and close to her, just as they were when they were living together in Aljustrel. She said she's thrilled with their beatification.

" 'Even though Jacinta and Francisco were just children, they reached an extraordinary degree of spiritual maturity,' she said. 'Mary gave them the grace to comprehend the spiritual significance of prayer and penance.' She recalled many of the little stories that I already told."

"Tell them again."

"Gladly. Jacinta loved grapes. When her mother would give them to her, she eagerly devoured them. But her attitude changed after the apparitions.

" 'When there were grapes and her mouth was watering,' my aunt said, 'she would say to me, "Let's not eat them. Let's offer this as a sacrifice for sinners." She would always give them to some other children or to the poor. She was always the first to suggest that we make sacrifices or do mortification for the salvation of sinners.'

"Lucia also remembered that when she was sick, Jacinta used to say to her, 'My head hurts a lot and I'm very thirsty. But I don't want to drink anything. I want to suffer for sinners.'

" 'When I used to go and visit her before stopping by the church, Jacinta would say, "Tell the Hidden Jesus that I wish him well and that I love him a lot." Or, "Tell Jesus that I send him many greetings."

" 'When I would console her on her sickbed, she would say, "Go see Francisco now, and I'll make the sacrifice of being alone." When Francisco was dying, Jacinta told him, "Dear brother, give the Lord and the Blessed Mother my greetings, and tell them that I will suffer everything they want me to suffer for the conversion of sinners." ' "

"What does she remember about Francisco?"

"As regards Francisco, my aunt said that he was a very quiet boy. He liked to pray secretly and make sacrifices. He was in love with Jesus. One day my aunt asked him, 'Francisco, what do you like most: to console the Lord or to convert sinners so they don't go to hell?'

"He answered, 'I like to console the Lord the most. Didn't you see how Mary, even in the last month, seemed so sad when she told us not to offend the Lord anymore because he has already been so much offended? I want to console the Lord and then convert sinners so that they do not offend him anymore.' "

"Did you ask her what message the beatification of these two little children might have for the world?"

"Of course. 'An extremely important message for our time,' my aunt answered. 'A message that concerns the importance of Christian education and the influence that parents have in education.

" 'Francisco and Jacinta's parents were deeply religious and lived out their faith together with their children by praying with them. When a family lives out their faith in such a deep way, they transmit it to their children. Nowadays, life is organized in such a way that there are very few opportunities for parents and children to pray together. For this reason, the beatification of Jacinta and Francisco is important. It will draw the attention of believers to the problems of living out their faith together with their children, even if they are little.' "

She Arrived at Night

Fr. Valinho had some pictures in his hand.

"What are those pictures?"

"The latest photographs of my aunt. The sisters took them on May 31, 1999, when she celebrated her fiftieth anniversary as a Carmelite. She looks just like she does in these pictures—smiling and peaceful. She doesn't look as if she's ninety-two years old. We hope the Lord will keep her with us for a long time."

It was silent in the car. Fr. Valinho was thinking about his aunt.

"How many years has she been in that convent?"

"She arrived on March 25, 1948, and she hasn't ever left since then. It was the feast day of the Annunciation of the Blessed Virgin. The Sisters of St. Dorothy didn't want her to leave their congregation. Since they felt so bad about it, they didn't let her leave the convent in her religious habit. She had to wear street clothes.

"She moved to the Carmelite convent in Coimbra at night. Some friends of the family took her in their car, and she arrived at the convent at four o'clock in the morning."

"Did the Carmelites know who the new nun was?"

"Only the superior. Something funny happened in this regard. I knew the woman who was the doorkeeper at the Carmelites back then. She told me that the prioress told her that a woman would be coming for a visit that night.

" 'She gave me instructions to open the door and call her immediately when the woman arrived,' the doorkeeper told me. 'If I wanted, I could hug her and kiss her, but I was to call her right away.'

"The doorkeeper didn't understand. Why was she supposed to hug and kiss a stranger? The prioress had never told her to do something like that before for anyone else.

"When the car arrived at such an unusual hour, the doorkeeper saw a petite, poorly dressed woman get out. Looking at her, the doorkeeper said to herself, 'I don't have the slightest intention of hugging or kissing her!'

"However, as she passed by her, she felt a strong urge to approach her. She hugged her and kissed her. It was only a few days later that she learned that the woman was Sr. Lucia."

"When did you get to know her, Father?"

"At that time I was at the Salesian University in Turin, Italy. A few days after she entered the Carmelites, my aunt wrote me a letter telling me where she was. She told me that she was very happy because she felt she had found the right place for her.

"In 1946, before leaving for Italy, I went to the Sisters of St. Dorothy to see her. I spoke with her as I had normally done the many times I had visited her. She didn't say anything to me. But when I went to say goodbye, I noticed that she was unusually effusive. She hugged me and kissed me, which she had never done before.

"I thought, 'Maybe she thinks Italy is the other side of the world!' I remembered this for a long time. When she wrote me that letter from the Carmelites and told me that she was now in a papal cloister, I understood what was going on. That was the last time that she would be able to hug me and kiss me."

"When you visit her now, can you no longer kiss her?"

"No. Even though I can visit her and talk to her, there's always the iron grill between us. She's there behind it."

"What do you usually talk about?"

"She wants to know about our close relatives. She wants to know about the nieces and nephews. She's a very thoughtful and loving aunt. I also tell her about people who have asked her to pray for them."

"Do you think your aunt still sees the Blessed Virgin?" we ask.

"Yes, I personally think she continues to receive visits from the Blessed Mother. I sense it from the way she acts at times. Every so often, she begins to talk about a certain topic and she will continue to do so for months, every time I go to visit her. It seems as though she has to carry out a task that has been entrusted to her.

"A while back, she talked continually about unity in the Church. She kept saying that the various Christian denominations should be united. 'More things unite them than divide them,' she said. 'Our Lord and the Blessed Mother want unity.' I know from experience that when she uses such expressions, it means that she has been told that she should take an interest in that topic."

We arrived in Oporto. Fr. Valinho pointed out the road to the Salesian house where he lives, and we stopped in front of the entrance.

Fr. Valinho got out of the car and grabbed his cloth bag.

"Thanks for the ride."

He smiled awkwardly. Nobody likes goodbyes. After a slight hesitation he said, "Let's give each other a hug. It's been good being together."

21

THE SMALL BULLET
AMID THE GEMS

Before leaving Portugal, we stopped by the office of the rector of the shrine to pick up some photographs that had been promised to us. They were photographs of the crown that was made for the statue of Our Lady of Fatima.

It is a special crown that is very valuable because it is made entirely of gold. It weighs over two pounds and is adorned with 313 pearls and 2,676 precious stones. It was a gift from the women of Portugal to Our Lady of Fatima, and it is placed on the head of the statue only on the most important dates associated with the apparitions. It is kept under lock and key the rest of the year.

However, one additional adornment was added to that crown in 1982. It is not made out of anything valuable. Because of its mysterious and enigmatic significance, it is undoubtedly the most precious jewel in the collection.

It is a small bullet that was meant to kill Pope John Paul II. The nine-caliber bullet, which Ali Agca, a Turk, fired in St. Peter's Square on May 13, 1981, tore through the Pope's flesh, entered his body, where it caused devastating damage, and then exited his body and fell to the floor of the jeep in which he was sitting.

The little bullet is now in the middle of the crown. Its dark, opaque color provides a rather stark contrast to the brilliant shine of the pearls and other precious stones. When the crown is placed on the statue's head, the bullet is only an inch from the Blessed Mother's head. This instrument of death has now been tamed, vanquished, and rendered powerless, in the same way that the Virgin will crush the serpent with her heel before the night of the ages.

Looking at that bullet and recalling the story behind it, it is impossible to ignore some rather uncanny coincidences. On May 13, 1917, the apparitions of Our Lady began in Fatima; on May 13, 1981, the sixty-fourth anniversary of that event, Pope John Paul II survived an assassination attempt in Rome.

He Shot to Kill

It was a Wednesday. That afternoon, John Paul II arrived in St. Peter's Square for his general audience, as he did every Wednesday. He was crossing the square in a white convertible jeep, and stopped to shake people's hands and bless the little children. At 5:15 P.M., he stopped to hold a little girl in his arms, kissed her, and handed her back to her father.

Then two shots were heard. The pope collapsed and let out a cry of pain. His white clothing turned red right around his abdomen.

His blood gushed out in torrents. The driver of the jeep took off like a rocket to the nearest ambulance, which was parked next to the Bronze Door. Unfortunately, that ambulance did not have adequate resuscitation equipment on board, so the pope was transferred to another ambulance. Within fifteen minutes, he arrived at the Gemelli Clinic.

The would-be assassin, a young Turk of twenty-three named Ali Agca, fired from a distance of six yards and had aimed to kill. He fired two bullets. The first bullet wounded the pope in his right elbow. The second bullet hit the finger of his left hand and then penetrated his abdomen.

John Paul II was near death when he was taken into the operating room. His blood pressure had fallen sharply, and his pulse was almost imperceptible. The Holy Father was unconscious when his personal secretary, Fr. Stanislaw Dziwisz, administered the last sacraments.

When Dr. Francesco Crucitti, the chief surgeon at the Gemelli Clinic, made an incision with his scalpel, a huge quantity of blood flowed from the pope. In fact, the pope lost sixty percent of his blood due to internal hemorrhaging.

The surgery lasted five hours and twenty minutes. The surgeons removed twenty inches of the pope's intestines. Little by little, the doctors proceeded to repair the devastation that the bullet had caused, and they realized that an absolutely inexplicable miracle had occurred.

The bullet had followed a totally abnormal trajectory, as though someone had guided it so that it would avoid all the vital organs. It passed within a few millimeters of his aorta and narrowly missed his spine. If it had hit the pope's aorta, he would have been dead; if it had injured his spine, he would have been paralyzed. Neither of these happened. The bullet did not cause any permanent damage.

As the Pope later affirmed, "One hand fired the bullet, and another guided it."

An Impressive Coincidence

Ever since the event, Pope John Paul II has been convinced that it was the intervention of Our Lady of Fatima that saved his life. The coincidence of the attempt's occurring on the same day as the anniversary of the apparitions at Fatima made a deep impression on him. While he was in the hospital, he asked his aides to bring him various books and documents on Fatima. He wanted to deepen his knowledge of that event.

Once again he read the text of that part of the secret that has not yet been revealed, which the Blessed Virgin had entrusted to Lucia in 1917. It is very possible John Paul II found some explanation for the assassination attempt in those pages. We can deduce this from the fact that his interest and his attachment to Fatima have visibly grown since the assassination attempt. At the same time, though, he has not manifested any desire to know who ordered the attempt.

Meanwhile, the would-be assassin had been arrested. The Italian magistrates and the secret service agencies from half the world made investigations as to who was behind Ali Agca. They were certain that the young Turk had not acted alone.

Who had armed him? The Turks? The Bulgarians? The Soviets? The Americans? Even the Vatican made various attempts at the highest levels to find out.

The pope, however, did not want to know anything. When his friend and compatriot, Cardinal Andrzej Deskur, asked him why he was so detached from the whole matter, he replied without hesitation, "It was the evil one who carried out that act. The evil one can conspire in thousands of ways, none of which interest me."

On Sunday, four days after the assault, the pope expressed his desire to address over a loudspeaker all the people who were keeping vigil in front of the hospital, even if he could speak for only a few seconds. Referring to his assailant, he told them, "I pray for the brother who shot me, whom I have sincerely forgiven." Later on, however, he never took any interest in the investigation, nor did he wish to follow the trial proceedings.

A Trip to Fatima

John Paul II spent twenty days in the hospital. He returned to the Vatican for his convalescence, but shortly afterwards, on June 20, he was readmitted to the hospital, where he spent another fifty-five days.

Nonetheless, he immediately started to plan a trip to Fatima on May 13 of the following year, so he could thank the Blessed Virgin for the blessing he received. During the trip, he made it quite clear through his behavior, his words, and his official speeches (both in their content and the passion, force, and wisdom with which he gave them) that he had some precise ideas concerning the attempt on his life and the events at Fatima, including the famous secret.

Even before the attempt on his life, John Paul II had had a deep devotion to Our Lady of Fatima. In fact, he had been contemplating a pilgrimage to Fatima for some time.

Devotion to Mary has characterized the pope's entire life. At the age of ten, he was given a scapular of Our Lady of Carmel. "I still wear it," he admitted once when he recalled this event after he was elected pope.

While he was a high school student, he joined a little parish organization called "The Living Rosary." His motto was the Marian phrase *Totus tuus*, meaning "All Yours" or "Everything for Mary." This is the motto he wanted inscribed on his papal coat of arms.

During his lifetime, Karol Wojtyla had had many opportunities to experience the Virgin's constant protection in concrete ways. However, the assassination attempt on May 13, 1981, surely provided the "proof" he needed of any hypotheses that he had formed of which he was not yet totally convinced. It is possible to conjecture that the attempt was the impetus that John Paul II needed to consider seriously the contents of the famous secret that had never been revealed but that were very familiar to him.

As we have already noted, the secret has not been revealed. Over the years, however, various rumors have been circulating. Some people claim that the secret speaks about natural catastrophes, terrible nuclear incidents, and frightening, apocalyptic events.

For this reason, no pope has wanted to reveal it. The Vatican has always denied these rumors. Yet people in authority have made certain statements that have led people to believe that there might be some basis for them to a certain extent.

Upon closely examining John Paul II's pilgrimage to Fatima on May 13, 1981, one has the clear impression that the pope visited the shrine because he was convinced that the world was in danger. He clearly intended to do whatever he could to save it. The pope arrived in Fatima on the evening of May 12. Addressing the crowd that had assembled for the night vigil, he said:

"I want to tell you a secret. I have planned on coming to Fatima for a long time. From the time that the well-known attempt occurred in St. Peter's Square one year ago, I immediately thought, upon regaining consciousness, about coming to this shrine and offering our heavenly mother thanksgiving for having saved me from danger.

"I saw Mary's special protection in everything that was happening. In this coincidence—there are no simple coincidences in the plans of Divine Providence—I also saw a call, perhaps a new call, to draw people's attention to the message that was issued here through three shepherd children.

"I am here to listen once again, in the name of the entire Church, to the message that resounded sixty-five years ago on the lips of our common mother, who was concerned about the fate of her children."

When he speaks in public, the pope always weighs every word. In this speech, he recalled his own personal experience, the attempt on his life, and immediately connected it to the general meaning of the apparitions of Fatima, to the message that the Blessed Virgin gave to humanity through the three shepherd children.

In his opening statement, he expressed a "precise recognition" of the apparitions. In 1930 the bishop of Leiria, after having examined the events of Fatima at length, declared that the apparitions were "worthy of faith" and allowed the Blessed Virgin to be venerated there. During his trip to Fatima in 1967, Pope Paul VI had spoken about the "devotion to the Blessed Virgin that had originated in Fatima." Karol Wojtyla, for the first time, emphasized his certainty that the Blessed Virgin was present in the apparitions and his certainty that she was the one who gave her message to the three children in person.

That evening, the pope prayed silently for forty minutes before the statue of the Madonna on the site of the apparitions. Then he took part in the evening candlelight procession. An immense crowd was there with him.

A million people were there from every part of the world, singing hymns. Some were barefoot and their feet were bloody. Some were exhausted. Most were drenched from the rain.

"I have come, like most of you," the pope said, "with the crown in my hand, Mary's name on my lips, and the canticle of God's mercy in my heart. He has done great things for me, too!"

The Meeting with Sr. Lucia

On the morning of the thirteenth, before the ceremonies began at the shrine, he met with Sr. Lucia. In 1967, during Paul VI's visit to Fatima, the visionary had asked to be received by the pope, but he had answered that she should speak to her bishop. John Paul II received her and spoke privately with her for twenty minutes. Then he asked her to stay by his side so that he could have several photographs taken with her.

This, too, was a gesture of recognition. It expressed his desire that people take seriously everything that Sr. Lucia has said and written over the years. It almost seemed as though he were saying that he, now the pope, was finally in a position to know its real value after the assassination attempt.

During the Mass, which was attended by an immense crowd gathered on the square, he opened his heart and revealed all the thoughts and concerns that he had in his soul. These thoughts and concerns were very serious.

He spoke in apocalyptic tones as he never had spoken before. He alluded to imminent, terrible dangers. Addressing the Virgin Mary, he begged and pleaded with her, with an almost desperate insistence.

He expressed his sorrow at the rampant moral decay, the primary cause of humanity's moving away from God. "How can people not feel dismay," he asked, "with the spread of secularism and permissiveness, which have so seriously seduced fundamental values away from the moral norms of Christianity?"

Then, out of a desire to interact with the crowd and to offer himself to God and to Mary at such an important time, he abandoned his usual manner of speaking. He also abandoned any attempt to analyze society and the condition of the world as an observer or a pastor. He continued his speech in the form of a prayer, praying as one man among so many confused and bewildered people:

"Accept, O Mother of Christ, this cry laden with the sufferings of all individual human beings. The successor of Peter presents himself here also as a witness to the immense suffering of mankind, as a witness to the almost apocalyptic menaces that loom over nations and mankind as a whole."

He used the words "apocalyptic menaces." He used the exact expression that is found in Lucia's letter and in her "references" to the contents of the famous "secret." As Sr. Lucia had been saying for many years, the Blessed Mother was asking the Church to make an act of consecration of Russia to her Immaculate Heart.

For the various reasons that have already been noted, this consecration had never taken place. The universal Church had not been convinced of the validity of this request, so, in her infinite prudence, she had never acted upon it.

However, John Paul II obviously knew things that others did not know during his pilgrimage in 1982, which even he had not known before. Therefore, he finally acted upon this request for the consecration of Russia. He could not act in the name of all the bishops, because he had not had time to consult with them. Yet he wished to make the consecration, even indirectly, by including it in a general consecration of the world without ever mentioning Russia by name. He used a formula that made his intentions quite clear.

In a very sorrowful tone, he prayed to Mary for "the world of the second millennium that is drawing to a close, the modern world, our world today." Then he uttered the explicit formula of the consecration: "Embrace with the love of the Mother and Handmaid, this human world of ours, which we entrust and consecrate to you, for we are full of disquiet for the earthly and eternal destinies of individuals and peoples. In a special way we entrust and consecrate to you those individuals and nations, which particularly need to be entrusted and consecrated.

"Help us to conquer the menace of evil, which so easily takes root in the hearts of the people of today, and whose immeasurable effects already weigh down upon our modern world and seem to block the paths towards the future!"

"Evil seems to block the paths towards the future!" This is a powerful phrase that depicts a truly apocalyptic reality. John Paul II, an optimistic person and a fighter by nature, would have never said these words if he did not have a clear vision of imminent danger.

"From famine and war, deliver us!" the pope went on to say in his intense prayer of supplication to the Virgin. "From nuclear war, from incalculable self-destruction, from every kind of war, deliver us! For sins against the life of man from its very beginning, deliver us! From every kind of injustice in the life of society, both national and international, deliver us! From attempts to stifle in human hearts the very truth of God, deliver us!

"Accept, O Mother of Christ, this cry laden with the sufferings of all individual human beings, laden with the sufferings of whole societies.

"Today John Paul II, successor of Peter, continuer of the work of Pius, John, and Paul, and particular heir of the Second Vatican Council, presents himself before the Mother of the Son of God in her shrine at Fatima. In what way does he come? He presents himself, reading again with trepidation the motherly call to penance, to conversion, the ardent appeal of the heart of Mary that resounded at Fatima sixty-five years ago.

"Yes, he reads it again with trepidation in his heart, because he sees how many people and societies—how many Christians—have gone in the opposite direction to the one indicated in the message of Fatima. Sin has thus made itself firmly at home in the world, and denial of God has become widespread in the ideologies, ideas, and plans of human beings."

Chosen for a Mission

All this took place in 1982. The fall of the Berlin Wall and the fall of communism were still several years away. People only vaguely recognized that communism had spread its errors throughout the world and had destroyed entire nations, just as Mary had predicted back in 1917.

Indeed, the lives of more than a hundred and fifty million people had been sacrificed in the name of this ideology. People only vaguely recognized that, after the fall of atheistic Marxism, other atheistic ideologies would take its place and continue the destruction. Individuals needed help in seeking out the truth and in stopping the course of destruction.

John Paul II was not satisfied with words. On this particular day during his pilgrimage, he offered himself for the salvation of humanity. Francisco and Jacinta were only children, but they had suffered as martyrs. The Blessed Virgin had asked their prayers and sacrifices for the conversion of sinners, and they had offered themselves. Just as they united themselves to the suffering of Christ, so, too, did John Paul II.

Looking over his life, it seems apparent that he was chosen for an extraordinary mission from the beginning.

His birth took place amid some unusual circumstances. His mother, Emilia Kaczorowska, was very frail in health. In 1906, at the age of twenty-three, she became the mother of a baby boy, Edmund. She had a difficult pregnancy, and the doctors forbade her to have any other children.

In the autumn of 1919, when she was thirty-five, she learned that she was pregnant. The doctors told her that she should have an abortion. She did not listen to them.

Karol was born, a robust and healthy child, but she suffered the serious consequences that the doctors had predicted. She lived for another nine years amid suffering and serious health problems.

When Karol was ten years old, he was playing at the house of a friend. His friend wanted to show him his father's gun. Thinking it was empty, he pointed it at Karol and pressed the trigger.

The bullet broke into pieces in the air. The boy's parents ran to the room. Karol, pale and frightened, was leaning against the wall in the room. The plaster of the wall behind him was riddled with fragments from the bullet, but not one fragment had touched his face.

In 1944, Karol Wojtyla was twenty-four years old. The Nazis had invaded Poland. He was working as a laborer in a factory.

On the afternoon of February 29, on his way home after working a double shift, an army truck hit him and flung him into a ditch. The truck continued on its way. A woman witnessed what had happened and ran to his aid.

The young man, who had a large wound on his head, showed no signs of life. Nevertheless, she informed a Nazi official, who had compassion on him and took him to a hospital. Wojtyla spent two days in a coma and was miraculously saved. Afterwards, no one ever knew what happened to that woman.

Six months later, following a popular uprising in Krakow, Nazi troops combed the city, and eight thousand young men were arrested and deported to the concentration camps. Wojtyla was in his apartment. He heard the shouts and cries of those who were being arrested and the shots that the Nazi soldiers fired.

The soldiers searched the entire building. He heard them stop in the apartment next door and in the apartment above and in the apartment below, but they never came to his apartment. Once again he was miraculously spared.

In 1946, before becoming a priest, he asked to enter the Carmelites. If he had taken that path, he probably would not have become pope.

The archbishop of Krakow was opposed to his plan. He wanted Wojtyla to become a diocesan priest.

Two years after his ordination, Karol once again asked to enter the Carmelites. Once again he was refused. The archbishop told the superior of the order who pleaded on his behalf, "Karol Wojtyla is very much needed in the diocese of Krakow, and the Church will need him in the future."

Pope John Paul's vocation matured amid suffering and solitude. At the age of nine, he lost his mother. At the age of twelve, he lost his older brother. At the age of twenty-one, he lost his father.

He was alone in the world. He entrusted himself totally to the Blessed Virgin. It was then that he chose his motto, *Totus tuus,* total consecration to Mary.

In Poland, Karol opposed communism with fearless courage. He delivered thousands of young people from the influence of the atheistic regime. He supported the Church of silence. When he became pope, he intensified the battle and became one of the major architects of the fall of Marxism in the world.

"In the end, Russia will be converted," the Virgin said in Fatima in 1917. It is conceivable that on May 13, 1982, in Fatima John Paul II offered himself so that all this could happen. Some day in the future, perhaps, people will realize that he is the man who was at the turning point (certainly not a political turning point) and the prophet who swayed humanity to change its destiny. To quote his own words, there are no simple coincidences in the plans of Divine Providence.

The Pope of the "Secret"

In the third part of her memoirs, Lucia wrote, "One day we spent siesta time at my parents' well. Jacinta sat down on the slab on the well. Francisco came with me to look for wild honey among the thorns of a bramble bush on a nearby slope. After a little while, Jacinta called me.

" 'Didn't you see the Holy Father?'

" 'No.'

" 'I don't know how it happened, but I saw the Holy Father in a large house, kneeling in front of a table, crying with his face in his hands. There were many people outside. Some were throwing stones, and others were swearing and using obscene words. Poor Holy Father! We have to pray much for him.'

"On another occasion, we went to the grotto at Cabeço. When we arrived there, we prostrated ourselves on the ground to say the prayer of the angel. After a little while, Jacinta got up and called me, 'Don't you see many streets, paths, and fields filled with people who are crying out of hunger and who don't have anything to eat? Don't you see the Holy Father in a church, praying before the Immaculate Heart of Mary, and many people praying with him?'

"A few days later she asked me, 'Can I say that I saw the Holy Father and all those people?'

" 'No. Don't you see that it's part of the secret and that people will find out right away?'

" 'All right. Then I won't say anything.' "

These two episodes, as well as other passages containing Mary's words to the three children in Fatima, indicate that "a" pope is connected to the "secret." People thought that Jacinta's vision referred to Pius XII or Paul VI. But John Paul II's life, the assassination attempt in St. Peter's Square, and his subsequent actions in following years all lead us to conclude that the pope in these visions is John Paul II.

In December 1983, two and a half years after the assassination attempt, John Paul II wanted to meet the man in prison who tried to kill him. Bewildered, Ali Agca asked the pope, "Why aren't you dead? I know I pointed just right. I know that the bullet was devastatingly mortal. Why, then, aren't you dead? What is this that they're saying about Fatima?"

The pope answered him. We don't know what he said. But speaking to journalists immediately afterwards, Ali Agca said, "The pope knows everything." Later, during his trial, he asked the Vatican to make public the secret of Fatima, leading us to believe that there are elements in the secret that explain the assassination attempt.

Return to Fatima

On May 13, 1991, John Paul II returned to Fatima.

The world had changed. Many important events had occurred, including the fall of the Berlin Wall, the fall of the communist regimes in Eastern Europe, and the visit of the Soviet leader, Mikhail Gorbachev, to the Vatican. In 1984, the pope, in the name of the entire Church, had officially consecrated Russia to the Immaculate Heart of Mary.

Pope John Paul II's speeches during this second trip did not contain any apocalyptic overtones. Although he did denounce the world's moral laxity and encourage the changes that are needed, his words were characterized by peace and great hope.

"As I face the confusion that shakes the different continents, and as I face the imminent subversion of values that undermines humanity's absolute certainty and even the life of nations, I adopt St. Augustine's hope when the city of Hippo was facing assault by the Vandals and an alarmed group of Christians from his church sought him out. The saintly bishop reassured them, 'Don't be afraid, dear children, the Old World is not drawing to an end, but a New World has begun.' A new dawn is breaking forth in the sky of history, inviting Christians to be light and salt in a world that has enormous need of Christ, the Redeemer of man."

Is humanity no longer faced with apocalyptic danger? We do not know. One thing is certain, though. Under the spiritual influence of John Paul II and millions of people who are intimately united to him and who have prayed and suffered with him, the world has certainly begun to change.

The story of Fatima continues. The story that began in Cova da Iria in 1917 has not ended. With the beatification of Francisco and Jacinta during the Great Jubilee Year 2000, John Paul II wishes to draw our attention to these far-off events in order to let us know that they are still very relevant. The new millennium has opened under the sign of Fatima, in the name of the common mother to whom Karol Wojtyla has entrusted the world on several occasions.

CHRONOLOGY

1907
March 22: Lucia dos Santos, the daughter of Antonio and Maria Rosa dos Santos, is born in Aljustrel, near Fatima.

1908
June 11: Francisco Marto, the son of Manuel Pedro Marto and Olimpia di Jesus Santos, is born in Aljustrel.

1910
March 11: Jacinta Marto, Francisco's sister, is born in Aljustrel.

1913
Lucia makes her first Holy Communion.

1915
Lucia sees a figure of light on three different occasions while tending sheep with three friends in a place known as Cabeço.

1916
On an unspecified day in spring, while tending their sheep at Cabeço, Lucia, Francisco, and Jacinta see an angel who introduces himself to them, saying, "I am the angel of peace."

During the summer of the same year, while playing at the well near their house, Lucia, Francisco, and Jacinta have another vision of the angel, who tells them that he is the "angel of Portugal."

In autumn, Lucia, Francisco, and Jacinta receive a third visit from the angel, who appears to them holding a chalice and a host.

1917

May 13: While they are at Cova da Iria, located in the vicinity of Fatima, Lucia, Francisco, and Jacinta see a "beautiful lady" above a little holm oak tree, who tells them that she has come from heaven and that they should meet her at that same place at the same time on the thirteenth day of the month until October. That evening, upon returning home, Jacinta tells her mother that she has had a vision of the Blessed Virgin.

May 14: Olimpia, Jacinta's mother, consults with Maria Rosa, Lucia's mother, who still does not know anything about the visions.

May 15: Maria Rosa questions Lucia, who only tells her mother that she has seen a very beautiful lady.

First days of June: People in Fatima are gossiping about the visions. Maria Rosa is worried and takes her daughter to the pastor of the local parish, ordering her to confess that she made everything up. Lucia, however, refuses and says, "I did see her."

June 13: Second apparition of the Blessed Virgin to Lucia, Francisco, and Jacinta. The Blessed Mother appears holding a heart in her hand that is crowned with thorns. About fifty people are present.

End of June: Because of all the gossip about the visions throughout the area, the pastor of the parish in Fatima summons the three visionaries and their parents so he can question them. At the end of the visit, he says that in his opinion, they are not visions of the Blessed Virgin and that they could possibly be a trick of the devil.

Beginning of July: Reflecting upon the priest's words, Lucia feels she might be one of the devil's victims. A dream confirms this suspicion, and Lucia enters a deep crisis. She decides not to return again to Cova da Iria.

July 12: Lucia informs Francisco and Jacinta that she will not be going with them to the site of the apparitions on the next day.

July 13: That morning Lucia hides from all the people who have come for the apparition. Around eleven o'clock, she feels an irresistible force calling her to Cova da Iria. She is no longer oppressed by any doubts and goes to Francisco and Jacinta's house, saying, "Let's go see the Blessed Virgin."

At noon, the third apparition takes place at Cova da Iria, during which the three visionaries have a vision of hell. Mary confides an important secret to them and tells them, "In October I will tell you who I am and I will perform a miracle so everyone will believe." About four thousand people are present for the apparition.

Beginning of August: Artur de Oliveira Santos, the mayor of Vila Nova de Ourem in which Fatima is located, summons the three visionaries and their parents to a meeting with him on August 11. An atheist and a Mason, he is concerned about the large number of people who are gathering at the site of the apparitions.

August 11: Antonio dos Santos accompanies his daughter, Lucia, to the office of the mayor of Vila Nova de Ourem, while Manuel Marto goes without Francisco and Jacinta. The mayor wants to know the "secret," but Lucia does not reveal anything to him.

August 13: While Lucia, Francisco, and Jacinta are getting ready for their appointment with the Blessed Mother at Cova da Iria, the mayor of Vila Nova de Ourem abducts them and takes them to jail. A crowd of about seven thousand people is present at Cova da Iria. Precisely at noon, they hear the characteristic clap of thunder that precedes the apparitions, and many people claim that they see a ball of light descend upon the little holm oak and remain there for a minute before ascending once again in the sky.

August 14: Artur de Oliveira Santos questions the three shepherd children at length, who are still being kept hostage in jail.

August 15: The mayor accompanies the three shepherd children back to Fatima, and turns them over to the parish pastor.

August 19: The Blessed Mother visits Lucia, Francisco, and Jacinta for a fourth time, while they are tending their sheep in a place called Os Valinhos, and promises for the second time to perform a miracle on October 13.

September 13: Fifth apparition of the Blessed Virgin. This time she appears once again at Cova da Iria, and twenty-five to thirty thousand people are present. Once again the Virgin says she will perform a miracle in October.

October 13: The last "official" apparition of the Blessed Virgin at Cova da Iria. The promise of a miracle, which was reported by various newspapers, has attracted an immense crowd, estimated to number between seventy and one hundred thousand people. The miracle occurs and consists of a spectacular atmospheric phenomenon, "the dance of the sun," which lasts several minutes and is seen by all those present. Other people throughout Portugal also observe it, but no astronomic observatory records it.

End of October: Several people who have been asked by the bishop to question the visionaries arrive from Lisbon.

1918

October: Francisco and Jacinta come down with a type of influenza known as the "Spanish flu."

1919

April 4: Francisco dies at ten o'clock in the morning. The next day he is buried in the cemetery at Fatima.

July 1: Jacinta is sent to San Agostinho hospital in Vila Nova de Ourem for treatment, where she remains for two months.

July 31: The death of Antonio dos Santos, Lucia's father.

A small chapel is constructed on the site of the apparitions from the offerings that pilgrims have left behind.

1920

January 21: Jacinta goes with her mother to Lisbon. While waiting to be admitted to the hospital, she stays at Our Lady of Miracles Orphanage.

February 2: Jacinta enters Doña Stefania Hospital in Lisbon, where she is diagnosed as suffering from purulent pleurisy and osteitis of the ribs.

February 10: Dr. Castro Freire operates on Jacinta, removing two ribs.

February 20: At around ten o'clock at night, Jacinta dies at the hospital. Her funeral is celebrated the following day.

February 24: Jacinta's body is taken to Vila Nova de Ourem and buried in the family tomb of Baron di Alvaiàzere.

1921
June 17: Lucia leaves Fatima to be a boarding student at the school operated by the Sisters of St. Dorothy of Vilar, near Oporto.

October 13: Church authorities grant permission for Mass to be celebrated in the little chapel built at the site of the apparitions.

1922
March 6: The little chapel is destroyed by dynamite during an attack that is carried out by a Masonic group.

1925
October 25: Lucia, who has asked to be admitted to the Congregation of the Sisters of St. Dorothy, is sent to Pontevedra in Spain to begin her postulancy.

1926
July 20: Lucia is transferred to the novitiate in Tuy, Spain.

October 2: Lucia takes the veil and begins her novitiate. The apostolic nuncio in Lisbon visits the site of the apparitions.

1927

The Holy See grants the privilege of a votive Mass in Fatima.

1928

October 3: Lucia professes her simple vows as a sister in the Congregation of the Sisters of St. Dorothy.

The first stone is laid for the large basilica at the shrine in Fatima.

1929

The Blessed Virgin appears to Lucia in Tuy and asks for the consecration of Russia to her Immaculate Heart.

1930

October: The bishop of Leiria, the Most Rev. José Alves Correira da Silva, publishes a pastoral letter in which he approves devotion to Our Lady of Fatima and declares the apparitions worthy of belief.

1931

May 12 and 13: The first major pilgrimage of the Portuguese bishops to Fatima and the consecration of Portugal to the Immaculate Heart of Mary.

1942

October 31: Solemn closing ceremony of the twenty-fifth anniversary of the apparitions. Pope Pius XII gives a speech in Portuguese and consecrates the whole world to the Immaculate Heart of Mary.

1946

May 13: A pontifical legate crowns the statue of Our Lady of Fatima as queen of the world.

1949

December 21: The canonical process for the beatification of Francisco and Jacinta officially begins.

1951

October 13: Cardinal Tedeschini, a pontifical legate, closes the Holy Year at Fatima.

1956

May 13: The Most Rev. Angelo Roncalli, the patriarch of Venice and the future Pope John XXIII, goes to Fatima to preside at the twenty-fifth anniversary of the consecration of Portugal to the Immaculate Heart of Mary.

1967

May 13: Paul VI's pilgrimage to Fatima, on the occasion of the fiftieth anniversary of the apparitions.

1979

The canonical process for Francisco and Jacinta is transferred from Fatima to Rome.

1982

May 13: John Paul II's pilgrimage to Fatima, during which he offers the Blessed Virgin the bullet with which he was wounded during an attempt on his life in St. Peter's Square one year before.

1991

May 13: John Paul II's second pilgrimage to Fatima.

1999

April: The process for the beatification of Francisco and Jacinta concludes by recognizing a miracle obtained through their intercession.

October 13: The bishop of Leiria, the Most Rev. Serfin Ferreira, announces at Fatima that Francisco and Jacinta will be beatified in the year 2000.

2000

May 13: The beatification ceremony for Francisco and Jacinta takes place in Fatima.